MW01227542

Playing the TRUMP Card

As America's Civil War Continues

Daniel Wilson

Azure Sol Publishing

PLAYING THE TRUMP CARD

KDP ISBN: 979-8-63254-390-3

Cover Design: Daniel Wilson

Azure Sol Publishing

5680 Fairfield Road

Fairfield, PA 7320

www.TheASKForce.com

Scripture versions referenced:

ISV	International Standard Version
KJV	King James Version
NAS	New American Standard
NET	New English Translation
NIV	New International Version
NLT	New Living Translation

~~~~ ~~~~~ ~~~~~ ~~~~~

To the only wise God and true Founding Father of these United States of America.

May the words I present be an honor to You and to those You have called for this time. Please be glorified in the pages of this book and in the hearts of the readers.

~~~~ ~~~~~ ~~~~~ ~~~~~

Table of Contents

Acknowledgements

Thank you to the many friends, family and supporters of this work. I can truly say that I would not have been able to complete this work without you.

I would like to specifically thank my bride, Robin Kasten Wilson for her selfless support and patience as I took her husband and companion away for months during this writing. Thank you for your professional edits as we put this manuscript together, but more importantly, than you for your unselfish love and support in my writing adventure!

Thank you too for my son-in-law Rocko Purvis for providing your excellent insights on my first draft. I know it was a painful task, but your thoughts were a great help throughout.

I would also like to thank a few other exceptional mentors in my life (though I'm sure they don't know they are), starting with Vice Admiral Donald Hagen, Jr. (the Navy Surgeon General during my latter days in the Navy). Just having your quick read and thoughts on specific aspects meant the world for me. Thank you. Colonel (Dr.) David Balt, my best friend and brother, thank you for your encouragement and insights. Our discussions began my thoughts about this book and having your support and prayers will always be one of my greatest treasures. Finally, Lt Col Laszlo Pasztor of Carlisle, PA - thank you so very much for your detailed review, insights and guidance. As an Army and community leader, your pointed challenges and recommendations took my thoughts to a much greater plain of professionalism. Thank you!

To my readers. Thank you for giving me the chance to express my thoughts and hopes about this magnificent nation to which I was born and am blessed to serve. It's your prayers that have upheld this magnificent experiment, and your patriotic efforts that will support its survival and purpose on this orb we call home.

May my words written here honor the Creator of all things…

Introduction

Is the American experiment approaching her prophetic *END* as foretold by President Lincoln? Are *We the People* on our final walk towards the gallows of our own making? Let's hope not!

For one of my 2016 podcasts of *America's Champions*, I felt compelled to research the meaning behind the *names* of our Presidential candidates, and my findings were truly Providential. For now, let's consider the more significant name for the moment - **Donald Trump** or *King of Wildcards*!

I'm sure you'd agree with me that this *King of Wildcards* has been playing his hand like few could have ever imagined. His Administration often reflects the operations of one of his casinos more than the most powerful governmental body the world has ever known. Yet elect him we did, knowing that he was a brazen gambler and caustic leader. I doubt we were alone in his election. No, I'm not talking Russia, China or other world power being involved in our electing the King of the Wildcards but something much more powerful. Yes, I'm confident there was interference in our 2016 elections and believe the 2020 elections will have the same.

As I'll reveal in the pages to follow, even if the deck had been stacked for our 2016 elections, a greater hand had reshuffled the deck in a way that would reveal the hand and heart of every player at the table whether it be a cheat, bluffer or a high roller. It has also revealed those who've been betting above their means as well as those in the gallery who may have had a cheating hand in the play. While the dealing isn't over, as the 2020 elections will reveal, the stakes and tempers continue to rise, and we the spectators fearfully watch every hand knowing that certain players would rather overturn the table than to play the hand they've been dealt.

While *Lady Liberty* takes what may be the final steps on the path to her self-made gallows, my hope is that our nation has not been abandoned to her self-destructive fate but that an amazing rescue is prepared for this *Land of the Free and Home of the Brave*. Though our nation is divided, I remain confident that *We the People* still have a hand in the game and can help determine our own future. The question is, do we continue to play the *TRUMP card* or do we fold? I believe the 2020 hand will determine the future of these United States and the world!

Playing the TRUMP Card

As America's Civil War Continues

(DOWNLOAD THE E-VERSION TO SEE IT IN LARGER PRINT AND COLOR)

Chapter 1 – The Lincoln Prophesy

God grant, that not only the Love of Liberty, but a thorough Knowledge of the Rights of Man, may pervade all the Nations of the Earth, so that a Philosopher may set his Foot anywhere on its Surface, and say, 'This is my Country. Benjamin Franklin – 1789

Righteousness makes a nation great, but sin diminishes any people. Proverbs 14:34 – ISV

~~~~~

A. S. K. America (published in 2016) was an attempt on my part to help right the ship, come around, and put our nation back on course. At the time of printing, I had limited insights on the candidates themselves but knew it was would be a significant election for our country. Mr. Trump had just thrown his hat in the ring, and Senator Sanders was building-up steam against Secretary Clinton. Of the Republicans who were on the campaign and the battle between Clinton and Sanders, I foresaw a tight election at both the Primary and National levels. To be honest, the result was a huge surprise to me, though my prayer throughout was for Providence to do whatever was necessary to heal our nation. I was certainly worried, and with the *Wild Card* thrown into the game, my concerns became even greater.

Shortly after releasing A. S. K America and the 2016 Primaries, I came up with the idea to see how the *names* of our Presidential Candidates matched their campaigns. Amazingly, most seemed a near perfect match. Here are the "Final-Four":

Bernard Sanders = Bear – Defense (Russian)
Hillary Clinton = Hilarious – Cliff (Gaelic)
Rafael (Ted) Cruz = God Heals – Cross (Hebrew/Latin)
Donald Trump = King – Wildcard (Gaelic/U. S.)

Of course, there are various origins and meanings for pretty much any name or word, so I've obviously selected the term that best fits the individual's history and their agenda. My intent to share this concept up front was to suggest that no matter what you believe about a *Higher Power*, there's no denying that the 2016 Presidential Elections were no coincidence. The Democratic party caged the *Defending Bear* while pushing the nation towards a *Hilarious Cliff*. The Republican Party, on the other hand, rejected *Healing by the Cross* and opted instead for the *King of Wildcards*. Could anything be more apropos?

So here we are rushing headlong into another Presidential election year (2020) with the *King of Wildcards* throwing card after card on the table, and other players within our nation and around the globe declaring the *King* is bluffing and is a cheat! Of course, the media continually challenges the King, while he repudiates the media and any who confront him. Those of us watching the game are like the spectators in a smoke-filled saloon keeping a wary eye on the table while our fingers lightly play with whatever weapons we have at our side. It seems that everyone is ready for a firefight at this *less than O. K. Corral* we call America.

We are certainly living in the most dangerous period in recorded time, yet it appears that *Providence* not only acknowledges the game at hand but is actively dealing the cards. My hope and prayer is that humanity is not playing her final hand, but that the change of decks and reshuffle were meant to reveal the players at the table and their character. Hopefully, *Providence* has greater plans for this *shining light on the hill* and for the world we humans have been put in charge of.

Here's the landscape of our nation as defined nearly 200 years ago by the amazing French author and philosopher Alexis de Tocqueville - *"America is great because America is good. If America ever ceases to be good, America will cease to be great"*. He then goes on to reveal an even deeper truth that *"Liberty cannot be established without morality, nor morality without faith"*. - Democracy in America, 1831.

Though we can argue this point for a millennia, I believe the United States was designed as a *light on the hill* shining hope and freedom of opportunity to all nations willing to open their eyes and receive the wisdom that our founders had so openly shared. It's a light that reflects the plan of the *Creator* for all mankind, although at our nation's onset, there were those intent to extinguish the light and control the masses for self-gain.

Sadly, a few short years after de Tocqueville shared the truth of America's goodness and greatness, Abraham Lincoln painted a more ominous vision of our nation's future if we failed to remain *good*. His portrait of America was one that revealed a corrupt and selfish people rising from the roots of this grand experiment with a specific intent to manipulate and enslave others for selfish gain. His words still ring true today:

"Shall we expect some transatlantic military giant to step the ocean and crush us at a blow? Never! All the armies of Europe, Asia, and Africa combined, with all the treasure of the earth (our own excepted) in their military chest, with a Bonaparte for a commander, could not by force take a drink from the Ohio or make a track on the Blue Ridge in a trial of a thousand years. At what point then is the approach of danger to be expected? I answer. If it ever reach us it must spring up amongst us; it cannot come from abroad. If destruction be our lot, we must ourselves be its author and finisher. As a nation of freemen, we must live through all time or die by suicide." Abraham Lincoln, January 1838.

Obviously, Lincoln was referring to a simple failure in our nation's fabric that would allow a select body of individuals to twist our laws, weave division, and surrender our nation's power over to such a body. Generations that had been nursed on blessings and abundance while being nurtured on the gift of freedom, felt it their right to take life from those less fortunate and to enslave them for their own prosperity. *"Having a form of godliness but denying the power thereof"* (2 Tim 3:5, KJV).

Lincoln saw that such corrupt and arrogant disregard of our nation's founding principles would lead to a weakening bond of honor. When certain sects of *We the People* felt it their right to possess or control other sects of our national family by subjugating our laws and honor for their own desires, nothing else could remain sacred. As Lincoln suggested, such a nation could not long endure. His answer was to give his all in order to disrupt the intentional acts of the selfish. We are at a similar place today.

Yes, the *Party of Freedom* may have won our great civil battle, but we have yet to win the war. Slavery has sadly endured beyond the Emancipation Proclamation, the Civil Right movement, and into our modern era, continuing to tear at our nation's fabric. Though the visage of slavery has been well hidden within the folds of our nation, it has certainly permeated her ideologies and overcome her design. As a nation founded on the principles of nature's God and brotherly love, America continued to harbor and even empower those who deny Godly principles and the honor of their fellow man. Though President Lincoln saw some fruit of his sacrifice, he certainly understood that a challenging future lay ahead for this nation. The saddened face we see in his latter portraits reveals his understanding that the evils of man had not been defeated and that America was certain to see another great calamity.

My heart aches for President Lincoln and the burden he carried, yet I believe that Providence is still honoring Mr. Lincoln for his ideals, prayers and sacrifices. These prayers were not Mr. Lincoln's alone but of millions of Americans who gave their lives to free their brothers, including those of us who continue to fight for freedom to this day and desire a nation and a world where all are free to pursue our dreams as well. Here's a charge I believe Mr. Lincoln gave to America's citizens and those around the globe who desire freedom and truth:

> *"It is rather for us to be here, dedicated to the great task remaining before us, — that from these honored dead we take increased devotion to that cause for which they gave the last full measure of devotion, — that we here highly resolve that these dead shall not have died in vain, — that this nation, under God, shall have a new birth of freedom, — and that government of the people, by the people, for the people, shall not perish from the earth."* (President Lincoln, Gettysburg Address, 1863)

Chapter 2 – Our Nation's Cornerstones

*WE hold these Truths to be self-evident, that all Men are created equal, that they are endowed by their **Creator** with certain unalienable Rights, that among these are **Life, Liberty, and the Pursuit of Happiness**.* Declaration of Independence Preamble, *1776*

The foundation of our Empire was not laid in the gloomy age of Ignorance and Superstition, but at an Epoch when the rights of mankind were better understood and more clearly defined, than at any former period, the researches of the human mind, after social happiness, have been carried to a great extent, the Treasures of knowledge, acquired by the labours of Philosophers, Sages and Legislatures, through a long succession of years, are laid open for our use, and their collected wisdom may be happily applied in the Establishment of our forms of Government. George Washington, 1783

Because of God's grace to me, I have laid the foundation like an expert builder. Now others are building on it. But whoever is building on this foundation must be very careful. For no one can lay any foundation other than the one we already have, Jesus Christ. 1 Cor 3:10-11 – NLT

~~~~~

As de Tocqueville suggested, America and every great nation is dependent upon being "good"! What exactly does that mean?

Let me share what I believe defines *good* using the principle I've coined as the ***Four Cornerstones of Freedom*** on which our nation has been established. No, not baseball, beer, hotdogs and apple pie, though these are certainly good, but the foundational truths that define who we are as a sovereign collection of individuals. As with any solid structure, our *Four Cornerstones of Freedom* were established at the onset of our nation's design through our *Declaration of Independence* and *Constitution* (provided in full at the back of this book).

1. **Creator/God**
2. **Life**
3. **Liberty**
4. **Pursuit of Happiness**

These basic principles are foundational to most if not all my writings, radio broadcasts and in my every lecture. These four principles, if placed properly at the corners of any structure or organization (nation, business, team or family) create a straight and true construction that can weather nearly any storm. Let's look at these individually to better understand each:

Creator/God – I like the term Providence since it's somewhat non-religious but an acknowledgement of the Creator of the Cosmos (time, matter, dimensions and conscience). You may also like the thought of the *Guy Outside Dimensions (GOD)*. Anyway, our nation's founders certainly believed that Providence was behind the formation of our nation by their acknowledgement of *"the Laws of Nature and of Nature's God"* (Declaration of Independence*)*. This reveals the reverence for a power greater than man upon which our Constitution and laws have been established and are further sanctified within our First Constitutional Amendment, our oaths of office, and prayers preceding government meetings.

Though none can prove or disprove a Creator, I propose that the order of all things is beyond denial of even the most devout atheist. The Lockheed Martin F-35 Lightning II is a fantastic achievement of mankind (intelligent design) yet the Lightning II is rudimentary in comparison to the magnificence of the Bald Eagle. Created from two insignificantly small cells from two separate living creatures, the Bald Eagle's cells merge and morph into a living and self-sufficient creature, learning to fly on its own, pursue its own fuel, and then regenerating itself over and again. Thus, every living creature having *"seed after its kind"* and working in unison (Circle of Life) is beyond comprehension and affirms Intelligent Design!

Though the United States of America may not be a *Christian* nation by law, she was certainly founded on Judeo/Christian principles that reflects a reverence of other people and their religion as aspects of a benevolent Creator. As such, the Authors of the Declaration established this as the first Cornerstone on which our entire nation would be plumbed.

Life – Interestingly, our Founders felt it necessary to signify this aspect of existence as being the most important aspect of humanity. If life is tenuous or unimportant, what would anything we do matter? Though the elements of a human body are said to be worth $1 in today's market, the living being is priceless. Life must be cherished within society or that society will cease to exist. From the beginning, mothers have been willing to risk their lives in childbirth in order to perpetuate life through generations to follow. Likewise, men sacrifice their lives in battle for the lives of their family and future. Life is hope, not in just being able to achieve but in being able to live to see it! Any who willingly destroy the most innocent are evil and dark of heart.

Liberty – When Life and hope for a future exist, *Liberty* becomes the springboard that launches us into a life worth living. We can reach our goals and dreams if we have the freedom to pursue and to hold them.

It is within all creatures to expand and to thrive. Any limitation to these natural desires becomes slavery: a dog tied to a tree, a fish contained in a carnival bowl or child bound to an abusive life. Liberty that fits within the nature of God allows us to become what we were each created to be. Our Founding Fathers established *Liberty* as the 3rd Cornerstone (like the 3rd leg on a stool) in order to give balance to our faith and life. Liberty does not mean an ability to do/have all we desire, but to freely honor the faith and life of others within the laws of nature and man. Liberty is dishonored when one individual uses their liberty to destroy the life or liberties of another.

Pursuit of Happiness – Herein is the reward for establishing the first three cornerstones. It provides the confidence that you can pursue your heart's dreams and goals in order to achieve happiness in this life without fear. With confidence you can marry a best friend, create a good family, enjoy a desired profession, pursue opportunity or adventure, and/or follow whatever stirs your heart knowing that the desire is worthy of the pursuit. This Cornerstone is wholly dependent on the solidity and assurance of the other 3 Cornerstones. Pursuit is what defines us and our life's worth.

This final Cornerstone completes the foundation on which the walls of security and comfort can be built. Once a haven is established, a greater boldness ensues within the heart of an individual, community or nation, allowing for a safe return from adventures and travels beyond the walls.

This Cornerstone is also a common point of attack by others because it is the visible reflection of our other cornerstones. Those who pursue little are ridiculed for their lack, while those who pursue greatly are ridiculed for their flamboyance. Sadly, it's human nature to envy, criticize and even threaten others for their pursuit instead of encouraging and helping them along the way. Man's nature tends to diminish others and/or take what others have accomplished for his own happiness. This last thought is another reason to establish strong Cornerstones for the foundation of a solid structure. Misused or abandoned resources will be seized.

America is an example of challenges that come against all who boldly pursue happiness. While many beyond of our borders are envious of our nation's success, some within our own borders have adopted an arrogant entitlement attitude and condemnation for our nation, secretly hoping for America's demise. This latter group was Mr. Lincoln's concern and what challenges America today. Those spoiled by unearned opportunity become envious of those who leverage opportunity into success.

A failure point within humanity is the ability to place the Cornerstones out of sequence. Establishing a structure solely on the Cornerstones of *Liberty* and *Pursuit* creates a shaky façade at best. Individuals and communities that boast of their greatness while teetering on a one-dimensional platform like the sets of Hollywood, glued together with glitz, glamour and shaky supports, are quickly destroyed or dismantled by a jealous adversary. Those that become wealthy by chance (winning the lottery, discovering oil or inheriting wealth) often create this one-dimensional foundation and find themselves on shaky ground with many enemies and false friends.

Solid and honorable Cornerstones secure a people and allow confidence to spread hope and wisdom. Many Americans have either forgotten or misunderstand our nation's Cornerstones, yet Providence has been revealing the need to reinforce our core principles and renew the foundations on which our nation stands. I believe the *Trump Card* was played for this very reason. Although I'm uncertain as to how this card will be played or to what extent, my hope and prayer is that Providence will play the hand in a way that rescues America and returns her to her place as a *shining light on the hill.*

Chapter 3 – The Dealer

Let us therefore rely upon the goodness of the cause, and the aid of the Supreme Being, in whose hands victory is, to animate and encourage us to great and noble action. George Washington, General Order 1776

Ask and it will be given to you; seek and you will find; knock and the door will be opened to you. For everyone who asks receives; the one who seeks finds; and to the one who knocks, the door will be opened. Mathew 7:7-8, NIV

~~~~~

Most reading this book are likely to feel they have little power over the events of the world, our nation or even within their own family, but I must say, we are collectively a greater power than you may think. I believe we've each had something to do with our current state and will continue to influence the outcome of our future, or I wouldn't be writing this book.

During Jesus' famous Sermon on the Mount, thousands from around the Roman empire and beyond came to hear the message from this powerful Prophet. Those seeking his insights and miracles included Jewish leaders, Roman Gladiators, farmers, fishermen, merchants, doctors, shepherds, new mothers, grandmothers and every other walk of life. From the poorest to the wealthiest, the uneducated to the highly educated, each came seeking truth and hope in an uncertain world. Their prayers were the likely cause of Jesus' arrival!

The quote above from Mathew 7:7-8 is the foundation for my A. S. K. Series of books, representing the Ask, Seek and Knock within the sermon. On the surface, this simple statement captured in the Gospels of Matthew and Luke the physician (Luke 11:9-10) is one of the most amazing secrets of all Scripture. A secret that wasn't revealed for the Jews, Christians or church alone, nor as means to become spiritually powerful, but for all people in all aspects of life, spiritual and physical, from the smallest to the greatest. A bold statement you say! It sure is and one that if heeded could open the floodgates of opportunity for you, our nation and the world!

As we'll see later, I propose that every human ever created is a unique puzzle piece created by design and for the design of humanity. Yes, we are all created on purpose for a purpose. That's right, you are the only *you* ever to be created with your exact abilities, skills, talents and purpose(s). None have travelled the same roads of life and none will ever share your exact story, your dreams or opportunities. As I present in my previous book *A. S. K. for Purpose*, you alone will follow the unique path to what I call *the greatest treasure on Earth, your heart*.

Let me explain how this plays-out in the hand that *Providence* has dealt the United States through our *Trump Card* and why *you,* too, are a factor.

Jesus didn't reveal any new concepts but was expounding on insights provided in ancient truths. In this case, it was the critical truth given to the Jewish prophet Habakkuk as his nation was under siege by their cousins:

> *"Write out the revelation, engraving it clearly on the tablets, so that a courier may run with it. For the revelation pertains to an appointed time - it speaks truthfully about the end. Though it delays, wait for it, because it will surely come about - it will not be late!"* (Hab 2:2&3, ISV).

I first realized the importance of this scripture from Pastor Gerry Stoltzfoos in the pivotal town of Gettysburg, Pennsylvania. Gerry was raised as a faithful Amish boy in the beautiful Lancaster PA area, and was raised to become a successful farmer and carry on the family religion. But much like Father Abraham, Gerry received a call in his heart from God to leave the farm and the Amish lifestyle (difficult to do) and become a preacher to the world. His solid family background coupled with his keen insight on God's world has changed the lives of tens if not hundreds of thousands. Understanding Habakkuk was a key for his calling.

Here's my interpretation of this secret given to Habakkuk (and now you) from the Creator of the Cosmos, - *"I've given you a vision, so write it down in adequate detail, give it back to Me, and I will orchestrate the events necessary to see that it happens. Trust me and don't give up on the vision because it will happen right on schedule!"*

My belief is that God (Providence, Karma, Allah, The Force, I AM, etc.) plants and then nurtures visions of purpose within each of our hearts and that much like the Earth, some major event usually reveals that vision. Mind you (as I'll discuss shortly) since man's creation there has been an Adversary (Satan, Darkside, Karma, etc.) of such visions. An Adversary that always challenges our intended purpose. It all sounds a bit ethereal, and I wouldn't blame you for levitating yourself through this chapter if you're not *spirit* minded. But, if you believe that something more exists beyond our senses, such as extra-terrestrials, dimensions, ghosts and the sort, then you may want to continue reading this section to see if it helps you understand the unexplainable a bit better. No matter what any may call it, something certainly exists beyond the veil of our own existence, and that something seems to help or hinder your life of success and purpose.

Let's quickly combine the thoughts of Jesus and Habakkuk:

The Ask is simply an adequate vision that enables us to evaluate our heart's desire against the realities of our abilities, talents, enthusiasm and resources. Like designing a Dream House, establishing adequate details begins to create a mental vision that's easy to conceive: the size, location, color and shape of the structure. From that we can then work-up true concepts for mechanical, electrical, plumbing, IT and such, which hone our vision, giving us more clarity of intent and hope for accomplishment.

The Seek is where plans necessitate an investment. It's also where reality validates and/or challenges the vision, with both aspects being essential to establishing a more solid foundation of the desire. In the Dream House example, once the plans are drawn-up, there are added validations that must be considered such as costs of construction, availability of property, availability of resources, access to utilities and a myriad of other aspects. As we seek our vision, adversity (such as zoning and financing) and opportunities begin to reveal themselves at every turn, honing the design and construct into a quality product and achievable solution.

The Knock is obviously a culminating point of achievement. You wouldn't knock if you didn't think doing so would achieve the Ask. During the Seek process, we glean an understanding of what lies beyond the door and how we must enter the door. Hiring a contractor and landscaper for our dream house is a door. Using a Navy SEAL example, doors could represent a test for promotion or a necessity to apply a few pounds of C4 to blow-open a door or wall where a known enemy lies in wait on the other side. Knocking and entering the door to our Ask is determined throughout the Seek process. Going through the door begins the next Ask.

Christopher Reeve, a real Superman in my opinion, has aptly defined one of my favorite truths: *"So many of our dreams at first seem impossible, then they seem improbable, and then, when we summon the will, they soon become inevitable."* That statement is the reality of life.

To be honest, I knew little of Mr. Reeve other than in his role as Superman, and my perception of him was of a great looking guy who probably had life handed to him on a silver platter. After his riding accident where he broke his neck and lived the remainder of his life as a quadriplegic, that's when he became a real Superman in my opinion. He never gave up, and I believe his efforts are the reason behind many medical advances in the world of neurosciences today. He epitomized the *A. S. K. principle* and continues to change the world long after he has personally moved on from it!

The concept that *Heralds* are being sent to see that the *Vision* is accomplished is an amazing truth. Much like the Christopher & Dana Reeve Foundation that has hundreds of Heralds continuing to seek healing, prevention and cures for paralysis and other neuro-disorders, it's my belief that such *Heralds* are constantly sent out by *Providence*. The myriad of foundations, opportunities, ministries and pursuits in this life are great examples of such Heralds. Like an Olympic athlete who pursues the gold medal, he/she unknowingly calls the coaches, trainers, sponsors and parents to participate in the unbelievable task ahead. Such Heralds are an answer to the call of the vision.

Few (if any) achieve their goals fully on their own. As outlined in *A.S.K. for Purpose*, all have a *crew* that goes on the journey with them. These Heralds can be flesh and blood or spiritual. In the same way, our adversaries along the path to our treasure can also be physical or spiritual. Doubts, infighting, resentment and fear are certainly come into play against an objective. Conversely, hopes, prayers, encouragements and insights work in favor of attaining an objective. Though prayer is an aspect we don't fully understand, histories often point to *Providence* shuffling things around and assigning Heralds (some being angels) out to see that things are accomplished.

No one can prove or disprove the spiritual realm, and yet all believe in something more. The adage *"there are no atheists in foxholes"* is certainly a reality. Something within us suggests there's more beyond our senses. I've seen prayer bring someone who should have remained dead back to life, and I've seen evil within the meekest doing feats beyond explanation.

As such, I believe the results of the 2016 Presidential Elections were the result of the Hand of *Providence* vice interference from Russians, Ukrainians or other human endeavors (though voter fraud was and will certainly be at play within our electoral process. It's my belief that the election of the *King of Wildcards* was an answer to prayer.

While many in America were fearful for our nation, many others were on their knees praying for a miracle over an uncertain body of candidates. I believe the *Wild Card* was the response to the prayers of those on either side of the aisle who truly humbled themselves before Providence, seeking another chance for our nation. According to Scripture, tribes and nations who willingly sacrificed (murdered) their children and the innocent, were always destroyed. *Trump's* efforts have been to pull us from the brink of such destruction since his inauguration.

It's now up to YOU and ME. Search your heart for what you desire (Ask) as the best future for you and this nation and present that desire in detail back to *Providence*. Find a means to pursue your desires (like mine was to write this book) and to make something happen. As life presents both challenges and opportunities, trust that both are a ways to best prepare the door, and when it appears, knock loudly and enter boldly into the opportunity Providence presents.

When the Israelites were taken captive by Babylon and then Syria, Providence caused a young Hebrew girl to be chosen as Queen over what was then the greatest power in history. At the same time, an antagonist had grown to power whose life's intent was to destroy all Hebrews. Queen Esther's Uncle Mordechai asked the Queen to risk her own life to rescue her family with a profound question that I ask you today:

"And who knows whether you have not come to the kingdom for such a time as this?". (Esther 4:14, ESV).

Chapter 4 – A Grand View

There is no security on this earth; there is only opportunity. General Douglas MacArthur

*Hell is the knowledge of opportunity lost; the place where the man I am comes face to face with the man I might have been. A*nonymous

Now faith is the reality of what is hoped for, the proof of what is not seen. For our ancestors won God's approval by it... by faith [they] conquered kingdoms, administered justice, obtained promises, shut the mouths of lions, quenched the raging of fire, escaped the edge of the sword, gained strength after being weak, became mighty in battle, and put foreign armies to flight. Hebrews 11:1-2, 33-34, HC SB

~~~~~

So, what should be our ASK? Sure, we should all seek to <u>be</u> good, but is that enough? Is it not that we should also <u>do</u> good as well?

Bette Midler's *From a Distance* is a beautiful composition and song but somewhat misses the mark. Her concept that the *"songs of every man"* are hope, peace, friendship and harmony are honestly portrayed, as well as the reality of bombs, disease, hunger and war. Where I believe she misses the mark is her concept that *"God is watching us from a distance".*

Here's the great conundrum of life - creation, existence, destiny and pre-destination, versus free-will, choice and responsibility. Obviously, knowing the truth of these would mean we know the truth of life itself, yet we don't. It's my belief (theory) that we are each created on purpose for a purpose. While the Creator may *know all* and is *present in all*, I still believe that He somehow provides us each with choices and consequences of those choices. Being created in His image, though, means we, too, are **creators** forcing us to choose our path for life and to adjust it as necessary.

Going back to Bette Midler's song, life is made of hopes and challenges, pleasure and pain, peace and war, and all other opposing spectrums. Like a warm fire after being in the cold or a cool dip in a pool on a hot sunny day, humans need and appreciate challenge, conquest and change. Champions become champions only through opposition - it's that easy. Without such, what would be the joy in living?

Our true challenges are those within our own being – where we sacrifice honor for personal comfort or gain. According to Jesus, our duty is to give our lives (take up our cross) to accomplish our purpose of being able to serve others. Does God create such situations? I can't really say, but I believe He knows and allows such challenges, even to the point of grieving, so that we can become *"more than conquerors"* through Him who created and saved us.

Here's an example. God didn't give us the automobile but gave us the mind to create them (as creators). He didn't give us alcohol but gave us the ability to create it. It's our *free-will* that allows us to drink and drive while the laws of nature from mixing the two may result in a horrific accident.

It's also the Creator's mind within each of us to know right and wrong and to choose between the two. Though mankind often chooses the wrong (bombs, disease, hunger and war) based on our selfish desires, mankind also chooses right (hope, peace, friendship, harmony and healing) out of our love for others. We put seatbelts and airbags in cars and limits on drinking. We have police who monitor our roads and pub owners who monitor their guests. All of humanity (except the most handicapped) battle internally with right and wrong. We also decide if we will take that battle to the world. Hitler took evil to the world, but heroes from around the globe came against him and his armies in opposition.

Does God care? Absolutely! Does God weep for those in pain? Absolutely! Does God cheer for those who triumph? Absolutely! Therefore, in my humble opinion, God (or whatever you call Him/Her/It) is so close that as Jesus said, the Kingdom of God is within us (Luke 17:21). He's not *at a distance*, but within us and caring of our every action.

Here's another aspect that many question - in Genesis it says that the Creator placed Satan (Adversary) in our midst near the tree of knowledge (good & evil) as well as the tree of Life. Knowing all things, I'm sure it wasn't a mistake, nor was it a mistake that He wasn't around when the Adversary tempted the woman. Though I can't say I know His full intent, I am confident that He (all knowing) had a plan from the beginning: that all of mankind from that day to this was meant to pursue the mystery of life, choosing between good and evil, and learning His heart. Was there really a Garden and the temptation? Since I wasn't there and haven't seen video footage of the event, I can't say, but the concept of temptation and failure is a reality for all.

Does it earnestly matter if the Earth is 7 thousand, 7 billion or 7 gazillion years old or whether it started here or on another planet in another Universe? We are all *challenged* within ourselves and within the world to overcome what seems to be an evil (sinful) nature. Like our Founding Fathers who gave of their fortunes and sacred honor for the future of this nation, we too are called upon to give ourselves for our fellow man and all of creation.

> *"When I shut up the heavens so that there is no rain, or command locusts to devour the land or send a plague among my people, if my people, who are called by my name, will humble themselves and pray and seek my face and turn from their wicked ways, then I will hear from heaven, and I will forgive their sin and will heal their land. Now my eyes will be open and my ears attentive to the prayers offered in this place. I have chosen and consecrated this temple so that my Name may be there forever. My eyes and my heart will always be there."* (2 Chron 7:13-16, NIV).

The above was from God to Israel's newly appointed King Solomon (meaning Peace), revealing His continuous presence and heart with His people. These words weren't for Israel alone but for all who live in this world created by Nature's God. I'd suggest you read the Book of 2 Chronicles for yourself to see how this promise from God played out.

Lincoln knew through his studies of history and Scripture that some men would sell their souls for selfish gain and comfort, with many willing to sell the entire nation's future as well. Here's Mr. Lincoln's analysis of these evils:

> *"whenever the vicious portion of [our] population shall be permitted to gather in bands of hundreds and thousands, and burn churches, ravage and rob provision stores, throw printing-presses into rivers, shoot editors, and hang and burn obnoxious persons at pleasure and with impunity, depend upon it, this government cannot last. By such things the feelings of the best citizens will become alienated from it, and thus it will be left without friends, or with too few, and those few too weak to make their friendship effectual."*

Making America great again does not happen by bringing business back to our shores, a growing Stock Market, creating the most powerful military or even having the lowest unemployment rate. It happens by her people becoming virtuous, which in turn will establish a stronger economy, more honorable people, and greater opportunities. Humility, honesty and responsibility are what make a nation great. Establishing a world that isn't in a race to the heavens but one that brings heaven to Earth will give both us and our posterity the right to pursue our visions and to encourage others to pursue theirs.

Herein is the challenge for us confused mortals here on Earth – the *knowledge of good and evil*. I am amazed that there are those who angrily fight for a woman's right to kill her unborn child while they demand lenience for a convicted murderer or illegal rapist. Somehow, our nation's balance is wrong, and her people are split. Our understanding of good and evil, right and wrong is certainly dimming.

Like many others, I worry that neither our nation nor the world can be rebalanced without a major catastrophe, and yet I pray and strive to help divert such. My hope is that Providence won't completely remove His hand from our nation in order to *reboot* the game of Life on Earth. I believe that our prayers as a nation should focus on the *Trump Card* being played to rebuild our nation's Cornerstones and structure as designed by our Constitution and the visions of our Founding Fathers, that *We the People* would give our all to serve one another, and that we would elect honorable leaders that have a right and unselfish heart willing to do the same in order to avert the coming global catastrophe.

It's been proven that none are truly good, but I have confidence that it is not a requirement. The requirement is a *heart's desire to be good* while acting in as noble a manner as possible towards others while seeking to honor Providence. To be honest, failure is often the catalyst that brings the requisite humility which in turn allows for the greatest success. In a world where man can heal the planet and her people, our prideful and arrogant attitudes have instead brought self-destructive tendencies that dishonor our neighbor and the Creator. We must repent and reset our nation's Cornerstones or witness the devastating reset by Providence.

"The only thing necessary for the triumph of evil is for good men to do nothing." - Edmund Burke.

Chapter 5 – The Enemy's Strategy

To be prepared for war is one of the most effective means of preserving peace. George Washington

Knowing their thoughts, he said to them, 'Every kingdom divided against itself is laid waste, and no city or house divided against itself will stand.' Matt 12:25 ESV

Be sober-minded; be watchful. Your adversary the devil prowls around like a roaring lion, seeking someone to devour. 1 Pet 5:8 ESV

~~~~~

As an instructor with SEAL Team 5's Advanced SEAL Training Platoon, one of my favorite evolutions was Land Navigation (easy hiking in the quiet outdoors). Though GPS was available, we'd train with a map & compass using back-azimuths in order to pinpoint our current location and then map out where we needed to go. It's a simple task when reference points aren't obscured or the enemy isn't hammering your position. The same methodology is used in business, communities and nations around the globe. You must first identify your present state in order to determine the direction ahead.

After identifying your own location, you then identify your objective. Next, you determine the means to move forward always keeping in mind (and in plan), the situation, terrain, enemies and allies. With challenging visibility or security, understanding these variables at every moment is critical.

So, where do we as a nation stand? Where are we going? Who's the enemy? Who are our allies?

Throughout our nation's history, we've had a long-standing schism that pulled at the bonds of even the tightest of families and friends. This illusive schism has created doubt and distrust at every level of family and society within our nation, causing daily turmoil, mistrust and even hate. It has weakened our Cornerstones and the bond that held us together. It's a challenge that tears at the fabric of our nation.

It's my opinion that this same schism has occurred in families and nations throughout history as well and is the reason for continual battles around the globe. Here's a reflection of the battle for our nation's heart that was included in a popular 1971 American manuscript:

> *"Lest we forget at least an over-the-shoulder acknowledgement to the very first radical: from all our legends, mythology, and history (and who is to know where mythology leaves off and history begins—or which is which), the first radical known to man who rebelled against the establishment and did it so effectively that he at least won his own kingdom, - Lucifer."*

Lucifer is solely named in Isaiah chapter 14 and means "shining one or morning star". Here's the text:

> *How art thou fallen from heaven, O Lucifer, son of the morning! how art thou cut down to the ground, which didst weaken the nations! For thou hast said in thine heart, "I will ascend into heaven, I will exalt my throne above the stars of God: I will sit also upon the mount of the congregation, in the sides of the north: I will ascend above the heights of the clouds; I will be like the most High". Yet thou shalt be brought down to hell, to the sides of the pit.* (Isaiah 14:12-15, KJV).

This dedication to Lucifer in 1971 was by Saul Alinsky in his infamous work, *Rules for Radicals. A guide for revolution.* His premise:

> *"It is for those young radicals who are committed to the fight, committed to life. - Remember we are talking about revolution, not revelation; you can miss the target by shooting too high as well as too low."*

Interestingly, *Mr. Alinsky* was born in Chicago, Illinois and taught his theories and methods for anarchy at various colleges in both his own city and others around the Northeast. It's no wonder that Chicago is known as the most corrupt city in America and, therefore, the ideal location for such a *Community Organizer* to operate.

Barack Obama, also raised in Chicago, not only knew of Mr. Alinsky and his Rules but used the concept of "Community organizer" 23 times in his own 2004 memoir, *Dreams from My Father*. I'm going to step out on a limb here and note that Barak in Hebrew has two meaning, *"Flash of light" (similar to Lucifer) and "Blessing" bless/kneel)*, while Obama means the *"High Places"* (historical places to worship pagan gods). Interesting, eh?

Let's look at Alinsky's Rules (with my summary):

1. "Power is not only what you have but what the enemy thinks you have." Power is derived from 2 main sources – money and people. People are a self-replicating power.

2. "Never go outside the expertise of your people." It results in confusion, fear and retreat. Security gives courage to all.

3. "Whenever possible, go outside the expertise of the enemy." Look for ways to increase the enemy's insecurity, anxiety and uncertainty.

4. "Make the enemy live up to its own book of rules." Over playing the targets rules will over commit and overwhelm them.

5. "Ridicule is man's most potent weapon." There's no defense for irrational attacks. It simply wears the opponent down.

6. "A good tactic is one your people enjoy." Enthusiasm creates greater thought and action.

7. "A tactic that drags on too long becomes a drag." Don't become old news.

8. "Keep the pressure on. Never let up." Constant and changing pressure throws the opposition off balance.

9. "The threat is usually more terrifying than the thing itself." Fear and ego can imagine worse consequences than reality.

10. "If you push a negative hard enough, it will push through and become a positive." A violence response can win sympathy.

11. "The price of a successful attack is a constructive alternative." Always have a solution or answer to the problem or question.

12. "Pick the target, freeze it, personalize it, and polarize it." Isolate the target and deter sympathy. Go after people and not institutions; people hurt faster than institutions.

It's easy to see that Alinsky's Rules could successfully undermine any organization, community or nation, and that it's being implemented today in America with the target being our Cornerstones and Constitution. As Wikipedia provides, *"the job of the organizer is to maneuver and bait the establishment so that it will publicly attack him as a 'dangerous enemy."* According to Alinsky, *"the hysterical instant reaction of the establishment (will) not only validate (the organizer's) credentials of competency but also ensure automatic popular invitation"*. Is this not what we see in our media today?

You may not believe in a physical *Satan* or *Dark Side*, but you must admit that evil exists, such as the likes of Hitler, Stalin, Hirohito, Ted Bundy, and so many other demonic individuals roaming the Earth with an intent to hurt or kill. As Jesus said, *"The thief comes only to steal and kill and destroy;"* (John 10:10) which completely counters our 4 Cornerstones of Creator, Life, Liberty and Pursuit.

Interestingly, *Hillary Rodham Clinton* in 1968 wrote a college thesis on Alinsky referencing him in her own 2003 memoir (*Living History*) with admiration. Her actions post college have certainly been in alignment with Alinsky's Rules, and it's possible he may have given personal support. When you look at the dozens of questionable deaths and myriad of scandals surrounding the *Clinton couple*, you must wonder...

In my opinion, the Communist Manifesto, Alinsky's Rules, Obama's book and Hillary's book all align with one another and are counter to our Constitution and nation's Cornerstones. Mind you, Communism was the strategy for the working/middle class to revolt against the Ruling Class for political control by force. As a Republican form of government, America is controlled by the people (all classes) through established laws as a safeguard against the politically powerful, wealthy and elite. As such, the revolt in the USA would be by the political elite against the People (as we have seen).

Yes, I believe there is an adversary (Satan) of God and His creation and that he abides on this planet and in the hearts of greedy and evil people. Like *Lucifer*, individuals who seek to *exalt their throne above the stars of God... Yet shalt be brought down to hell* (Isaiah 14 KJV).

Such greedy individuals have found their way into powerful places., yet *We the People* remain in control of our nation through our *Cornerstones and Constitution*. Let's return our focus to these standards!

Chapter 6 – Corruption at the Top

Those who would give up essential Liberty, to purchase a little temporary Safety, deserve neither Liberty nor Safety. Benjamin Franklin

The most terrifying words in the English language are: I'm from the government and I'm here to help. Ronald Reagan

So the law is paralyzed, and justice never goes forth. For the wicked surround the righteous; so justice goes forth perverted. Habakkuk 1:4, ESV

*They promise them freedom, but they themselves are slaves of corruption. For whatever overcomes a person, to that he is enslaved.*2 Peter 2:19, ESV

~~~~~

This will be a sensitive and controversial chapter using some concepts alluded to earlier in respect of our present state. The Enemy (last chapter) has specifically staged himself within our America's political realm with the intent to derail this *One Nation Under God* with a primary intent to divide and conquer. As we try to regain balance while our nation is pushed-back on her heels, the enemy has pressed for greater division and manipulation from issues such as Russia/Ukrainian voting interference, Climate Change, Nuclear Catastrophe, ISIS, and now the Corona Virus and Market disaster. Sadly, we've taken our focus off those within our government who make daily decisions that affect our actual state of being while they themselves posture their futures through their power and our nation's resources for personal gain.

To me, there's a simple litmus test for identifying corruption – when a select individual, body or group receives special treatment, there's a corrupt intent attached. American's, particularly the middle class, are paying the bills for our leadership who use our tax dollars like Monopoly money. These wealthy politicians bribe and leverage quid pro quo using what we have struggled to earn. I can assure you, while candidates attack the wealthy from the podium, they have no intent of taking real tax dollars from their wealthy friends and financiers but simply divert our focus to others while their hands are in our pockets for their gain. The strategy is to leverage the taxes paid by the middle (working) class as a means to buy the votes of the lower (slave) class in order to join the upper (elite) class at the top. Mind you, not all politicians are on this wealth enhancement plan, but many are, and I can assure you, they're on both sides of the aisle.

A 2018/19 FBI study found Universities including Yale, Duke, Stanford and Wake Forest take more students from families in the top 1% of the income distribution than from those in the bottom 60% combined. The investigation proved that the wealthy (such as Trump's son-in-law) were given entrance into universities like Harvard and Yale where the parents were large donor. The FBI has also uncovered that legacy applicants (alumni family) at Harvard, Yale, Princeton, Georgetown and Stanford were two to three times higher to garner admission than others.

More troubling is the quid pro quo exposed in July of 2019 by Jeff Poor between senior U. S. Politicians and Ivy League universities. His analysis revealed that the children of President Obama, Senator Schumer, Senator Menendez, Senator Blumenthal, Governor Spitzer and Vice President Gore (all 4 of his kids) somehow each overcame the extreme admission standards to qualify, attend and graduate from Harvard. Poor says the odds of this happening is "like getting hit by lightning every day for a year". Obviously, these schools present the *elite of society* with special opportunities for their finances and future.

Another example of this is portrayed in Peter Schweizer's book "Secret Empires" (2018). In summary, after the death of Senator John Heinz of PA, his son Chris became the stepson of Senator John Kerry of Massachusetts. Chris Heinz (graduate of Yale and Harvard) joined forces with Hunter Biden (graduate of Yale), the son of Vice President Joe Biden, and Devon Archer (John Kerry's 2004 presidential campaign advisor), to establish Rosemont Capital, a $2.4 billion private equity firm co-owned by Biden and Heinz with Archer as *Managing Partner*. It's hard to trace the actions of this trio, but in essence, a *tree* of the partnership was Rosemont Seneca, which within a year after inception found the trio in meetings with the highest levels of Chinese leadership and making major deals with the government of China. Around the same time period, these corporate managers were working on other significant relationships with the governments of Ukraine and elsewhere.

Another example of questionable dealing at the highest levels of power was in 2011, the United States Postal Service (USPS) reported that it had a deficit of $billions. According to various sources, that same year Congress awarded an exclusive contract to one of the world's largest commercial real estate firms, the CB Richard Ellis Group (now CBRE

Group, Inc.). The challenge comes as CBRE's Chairman of the Board, Richard Blum, happens to be the husband of Senator Diane Feinstein of California. Mr. Blum is not only the Chairman, but his private equity firm, Blum Capital, is one of CBRE's larger institutional stockholders. An added example of Feinstein's insider manipulation was the recent off-loading of nearly $6 million in stocks immediately after a briefing on the COVID-19 pandemic, and just before the market crash.

I can't help but believe that there are thousands of "shady deals" that have gone on under the radar for members of Congress and within our top government offices. *Power corrupts, and absolute power corrupts absolutely.* Sadly, we'll never be able to identify most of these dealings, and many politicians who have become wealthy on the backs of American taxpayers will slip into positions of power elsewhere. You wonder how many members of Congress who quit shortly after Trump's election had shady dealings going on and decided to jettison in order to avoid being scrutinized or blackmailed.

Here are a few other thoughts that are even scarier: Peter Schweizer's book "Clinton Cash" (2016) revealed likely corruption on a global scale. He suggests that 85 of the 154 private interests who'd met with Clinton during her tenure as Secretary of State were Clinton Foundation donors. Schweizer suggested that the foundation served as a means for donors to curry favor with then Secretary of State Hillary Clinton. Emails eventually turned up showing how the foundation intervened to arrange a meeting between Clinton and the Crown Prince of Bahrain, a country that had been a major foundation donor. In another article, it's said that "a Chicago commodities trader who donated $100,000 to the foundation got a top job on a State Department arms control panel, despite having no experience in the area." In a November 2018, *Investor's Business Daily* had an article titled: *"Scam Exposed: Donations to Clinton Foundation Plummeted After Clinton Lost the Election."*

Here's what I believe is the most egregious and frightening example of high corruption in our nation. While the Federal Bureau of Investigation (FBI) under Director James Comey was basically slapping the hand of then Presidential Candidate Hilary Clinton for knowingly committing national security breaches and then intentionally destroying the evidence, he seemed to be plotting with Clinton on one of the most disturbing and costly corruption efforts in American history.

Beginning in late July 2016, a joint effort between the FBI, the Central Intelligence Agency (CIA), and the National Security Agency (NSA) under the Obama Administration began *Operation Crossfire Hurricane,* a counterintelligence investigation into links between then Presidential Candidate Donald Trump, his associates and Russian officials based on a paid Clinton/DNC foreign spy (Steele) Dossier that had been pushed through the Foreign Intelligence Surveillance (FISA) Court for surveillance of Trump's aide Carter Page.

This "Operation" had basically carried our nation along a wasteful path from 2016 through the President Trump Impeachment Hearings of 2020, spending hundreds of $millions in tax funds at the added expense of tens of thousands of man hours to subpoena, try and defend the false allegations. In my mind, this was solely an intent to stop our *Wild Card* from achieving his campaign goals and to retard the American economy for the 2020 elections. And it's my opinion that we're not through with this team's attacks just yet.

How would you feel if the most powerful forces in the world came after you and your family with the full funding and protection of the American government? That's what we've seen during these last four-plus years, to the point that a military hero and leader, Lieutenant General Michael Flynn, could be framed, accused and tried by the very nation he gave his all for. Our media quickly and boldly pointing-out that he is now a "convicted felon". Again, *power corrupts, and absolute power corrupts absolutely.*

We can't expect what we don't inspect!

To keep America *great*, we must keep her *good*. Benjamin Franklin challenges us today with this: *"Rebellion to tyrants is obedience to God".*

Chapter 7 – Mind Control

The real problem is that through our scientific genius we've made of the world a neighborhood, but through our moral and spiritual genius we've failed to make of it a brotherhood. Martin Luther King, Jr.

If you think you can or you think you can't, you're right. Henry Ford

You therefore, beloved, knowing this beforehand, take care that you are not carried away with the error of lawless people and lose your own stability. 2 Peter 3:17 ESV

Yet the righteous holds to his way, and he who has clean hands grows stronger and stronger. Job 17:9, ESV

~~~~~

How did we get to this place where evil is acceptable and good is targeted? Communications!

Communication is the most vital aspect of any society or endeavor. From family to military operation, communications are a key factor between success or failure, and always the primary target of the enemy.

In today's world, social media, network television, e-mail, news radio, movies, e-books, newspapers, magazine and so many other venues allow massive amounts of information (communication) to be propagated worldwide in the blink of an eye. A butterfly in Indonesia can truly change the course of business in America, and a single word from the right (or wrong) individual can initiate a shot heard around the world.

The **Associated Press (AP)** was established in 1846 during the presidency of James K. Polk, a Democratic protégé of Andrew Jackson (founder of the Democratic Party). Just preceding the Civil War, Polk was a champion for expanding both the U. S. territories and American slavery, following in his mentor's path. Expanding slavery, sequestering the Indians onto reservations (e.g. the *Trail of Tears*) and establishing a national media presence was his means of controlling the American landscape.

More amazing is that the **AP** has officially counted the vote in U. S. elections since 1848, including national, state and local races down to the legislative level for all 50 states as well as key ballot measures. The **AP** collects and verifies returns in every county, parish, city and town across the U. S. and declares winners in over 5,000 contests. As of 2016, news collected by the AP was published and republished by more than 1,300 newspapers and broadcasters. The AP operates 263 news bureaus in 106 countries and operates the AP Radio Network that provides newscasts twice hourly for various broadcast/satellite radio and television stations. (Wikipedia). Talk about power!

No big deal you say!

The truth is that a handful of individuals define the majority of what the western world hears and sees, not so different than Communist regimes where the government controls all media venues. Like an intravenous infusion, the AP's narrative is infused into our very being through 24-hour news, talk shows, radio programs, newspaper and the various social media outlets. Thankfully there are a few who challenge the intended mantra, though such challenges are very limited and constantly attacked. Many western nations have few filters on their targeted propaganda. If you hear the same *jingle and verbiage* on literally dozens of venues (Fox News included), it's certain to be a pushed agenda from the AP. ***Perception is reality.***

And there's more! Both the **Public Broadcasting Service (PBS)** and **National Public Radio (NPR)** were established under another Democratic President in 1967, Lynden B. Johnson.

> **PBS** has more than 350-member television stations, many owned by educational institutions, nonprofit groups (affiliated with local public-school district or collegiate educational institution), or entities owned by or related to state government.

> **NPR**, with a syndication of over 1,000 public radio stations in the United States differs from other non-profit membership media organizations in that it was established by an act of Congress. Most of its member stations are owned by government entities (often public **universities**).

> An example of the benefactors for AP, PBS ad NPR is the October 2010 $1.8 million grant from the Open Society Institute founded by business magnate and Hedge Fund manager George Soros. Follow the money, and you'll see who powers our broadcasting standards.

A recent seizure of American communication programs was the **Obama Phone.** Yep, another Democratic move in controlling communications.

Leveraging the Telecommunications Act of 1996, President Obama used the Universal Service Fund (paid by our cell contracts) to put free phones into the hands of low-income voters, typically those who are on Welfare (**www.Obamaphone.com/**). Each phone was pre-loaded with specific applications to direct the user towards an intended communication venue. Not only are the phones paid for by those who pay for their own plan, these same taxpayers pay for the marketing and advertising of these phones and plans to ensure that unemployed Welfare recipients get their communication venue.

Of course, nothing is free…so one must wonder what the quid pro quo return would be. Obviously, for those with nothing else to take, they simply require a vote to ensure a continued handout.

Another significant communications maneuver during the Obama Administration was the final surrender of Internet oversight by the United States, relinquishing Internet Protocols to the *Internet Corporation for Assigned Names and Numbers* (ICANN), a California based non-profit entity presently headed by CEO/President Göran Marby of Sweden, with Chairman of the Board, Cherine Chalaby of the Netherlands. Yep, the entire internet (created by the U. S.) was handed over by Obama to the United Nations.

In 1984, George Orwell realized an amazing truth - ***"He who controls the past controls the future, and he who controls the present controls the past."*** This was hugely evident over the last 10 years as I researched our ". Gov" web sites for historical data and graphics. During the Obama Administration, nearly every ".gov" site I hit lead to a promotion of the Obama agenda and program. Over the last 10 years, it has been nearly impossible to link to an actual historical document or graphic without being redirected to an Obama smile, quote or promotion.

On July 16th of 2019, the Senate Subcommittee on the Constitution held a hearing titled ***"Google and Censorship through Search Engines"***. With Senator Rafael Cruz presiding as Chairman, he had a keynote witness named Dr. Robert Epstein, a Senior Research Psychologist at the American Institute for Behavioral Research and Technology in Vista CA, and former editor-in-chief of *Psychology Today*. In testifying, Dr. Epstein described himself as a strong Democrat and "vocal public supporter" of Hillary Clinton. Epstein testified that in the 2016 election, *Google* generated between 2.6 million (to as high as 10 million) votes for Clinton through deceptive manipulation of search results. He warned that if, in 2020, companies like Google and Facebook all support the same presidential candidate, they could easily affect up to **15 million votes** or more.

I believe that number is low considering Facebook, Google, Twitter and many other media venues not only manipulate their product to oppose specific candidates while favoring their own, but they also donate hundreds of $millions into campaigns and Super Political Action Committees (PACs) for their favored candidates. According to a Nov 2, 2016 Washington Post article, out of the top 10 political donors, 6 are Hedge Fund Managers and 2 are media moguls. The only Republican is a Casino magnate. In the list are the co-creators of Facebook, Dustin Moskovitz & Carl Tuna while Zuckerberg is somewhat off the radar but an absolute player (all Democrats). Though it's hard to pin a donation profile on Google/Alphabet Inc. (understandably), it appears that over 80% of their tens of $millions in political donations went to Democratic candidates.

No. ⬦	Name ⬦	Net worth (USD) ⬦	Age ⬦	Nationality ⬦	Source(s) of wealth ⬦
1 —	Jeff Bezos	$131 billion ▲	55	United States	Amazon
2 —	Bill Gates	$96.5 billion ▲	63	United States	Microsoft
3 —	Warren Buffett	$82.5 billion ▼	88	United States	Berkshire Hathaway
4 —	Bernard Arnault	$76 billion ▲	70	France	LVMH
5 ▲	Carlos Slim	$64 billion ▼	79	Mexico	América Móvil, Grupo Carso
6 —	Amancio Ortega	$62.7 billion ▼	82	Spain	Inditex, Zara
7 ▲	Larry Ellison	$62.5 billion ▲	74	United States	Oracle Corporation
8 ▼	Mark Zuckerberg	$62.3 billion ▼	34	United States	Facebook
9 ▲	Michael Bloomberg	$55.5 billion ▲	77	United States	Bloomberg L.P.
10 ▲	Larry Page	$50.8 billion ▲	45	United States	Alphabet Inc.

Forbes 2019 List of the World's Wealthiest

BTW - Hedge Funds are a collective group of investors (the wealthiest in society) who not only ride the wave of the market but manipulate the market each day based on intentional narratives pushed through "their" social media venues. It's an interesting thought that those who control the news have such a dynamic link to those who control the market and that these billionaires have a shared passion in politics. Included in this effort are the many wealthy movie stars (media magnets). As the Corona Virus panic and Stock Market roller coaster hit America and the world, it's easy to see the resulting manipulation and power grab by the most liberal of our stars and elite. *He who has the gold makes the rules while he who makes the rules takes the gold.*

Here's the most disturbing thought! Had the *Hilarious Cliff* (Clinton) been elected in 2016, it's my belief that **Barack Hussain Obama** would be sitting in the only position more powerful than the White House - the **Secretary of the United Nations**! So, while the Clinton regime ran the United States, Mr. Obama would run the United Nations and basically the world. There's no doubt that our nation was teetering and is even now teetering on oblivion. This "Invisible Enemy" that the *Trump Card* continually acknowledges isn't COVID-19 but the wealthy and politically elite who are trying to destabilize the world in order to regain control. Don't doubt me, Obama and Clinton want their power back while Joe Biden is the malleable entity that can give it to them.

Proof for this concept was provided in the recent PBS (Democrat media venue) Frontline 2020 Election documentary by Michael Kirk and his team, *"America's Great Divide: From Obama to Trump."* I'd recommend watching this documentary to understand the continuing agenda that boldly promotes Mr. Obama, while tarnishing everything Conservative and Trump. The intent is obvious: to further divide our nation using the Black vs White, Left vs Right and Poor vs Wealthy cards. Playing the **Victim card** is certainly a powerful means to draw-in the weak minded, while our richest Americans who control the media and the Market, are using their power, control and wealth to implement the Alinsky model.

The question is how and when does the *Trump Card* get played, and will it mean anything? ***Power and Profit*** are always the bottom-line.

Chapter 8 – Dysfunction at Home

Family is not an important thing. It's everything. Michael J. Fox

Of all nature's gifts to the human race, what is sweeter to a man than his children? Marcus Tullius Cicero

People will not look forward to posterity, who never look backward to their ancestors. Edmund Burke

The father of a righteous child has great joy; a man who fathers a wise son rejoices in him. Proverbs 23:24, NIV

~~~~~~

How does a nation of supposed "evolving" people find themselves in a place where they can so easily be manipulated by external influences such as those noted in the last chapter? Where is our common sense and collective wisdom? Let's look at the family of mankind and see if we can make some sense of it all.

Mitochondrial DNA (mtDNA) studies from around the globe have basically concluded that humanity today has a single ancestor. Though studies are still limited and can't adequately decipher dates beyond written history, they have identified a basic starting point which is near Africa or the Middle East. Interestingly, studies have traced the earliest writing back to around 3,000 BC with Mesopotamia (Eastern Turkey/Norther Iran) seeming to be the oldest and Egyptian being soon after. Both locations are wholly supported by the concept of Noah and his family migrations while also being the general area identified by most mtDNA studies of our earliest ancestors.

So, my theory is that Noah and his family were much more advanced than we give them credit for today. Most depictions show them as long haired, robe wearing, illiterate zookeepers who had no knowledge of their ship or circumstances. It's my firm belief they were survivors of an advanced human civilization, much like ours today, that understood the basics of science, mathematics and the written word. It's also my added belief that some ancient artifacts found today that stump our scientific understanding were established before the flood, such as the pyramids around the world and some metals and other artifacts.

Imagine loading your immediate family and hundreds of paired animals on a floating boat knowing that all of civilization would be destroyed! You wouldn't take your cell phone or computer, but as much food, seeds, and hand tools as you could. Advanced technology would have no value in a wiped-out world without electricity or internet. No matter the level of their technological skills, this family spent most of their life making and loading the Arc, and upon landing, their focus would obviously be on survival and comfort, while focusing on little more than the creation of wine and beer that would help them cope with the magnitude of their losses and new situation.

So written history and artifact validation tends to put Noah to around 3,000 BC. While mtDNA studies remain indecisive on when our species originated (how could they know), most still agree that man began less than 20,000 years ago, that we all came from a single couple, and then dispersed around the globe. But the Noah story is not alone:

> The Hawaiian story is of Nu'u, who built a boat with which he escaped a Great Flood, landing on Mauna Kea on the Big Island. Kae is said to be the creator god, descended to earth on a rainbow.

> The Chinese legend of Gun-Yu (Great Flood) is said to have occurred during the reign of Emperor Yao (3,000 BC), and has been validated by archaeologists researching the Yellow River.

> The Mesopotamian (Persian) story of Gilgamesh, who reigned around 2700 years BC, includes detailed stories of a great flood as validated by artifacts associated with Aga and Enmebaragesi of Kish, two other kings named in the stories.

> Babylon and Egypt each have similar legends - Babylonian having ten kings (Pitris in Hindu) that ruled before a great flood and saving the Seven Apkallu - Egypt having 10 Shining Ones that ruled before the Great Deluge, with the hero Toth, who saved himself and the Seven Sages.

During a trip to Northern California last summer, Robin and I stopped in at the Hupa Tribe Museum where we met a great young man named *Silas Chitawn Jackson*. Silas is being groomed as the tribe historian and future tribal leader, and as such he knew much about the museum artifacts and could speak the language of his ancestors perfectly. As we chatted, Silas explained that "all" Native American tribes have a flood story. His tribes story is about a man named *Naa tini hwey* (again, sounds like Noah) who legend says floated in a giant basket upon the waters of a great flood with his small family to establish all native tribes of the American Continent. As Silas shared the story in his native language, I could almost see his great grandfather of hundreds (maybe thousands) of years ago telling the story to his family over a fire in a teepee. Awesome!

It really doesn't amaze me that hundreds of historical writings and accounts, archeological finds, and mtDNA validations confirm the concept of someone called Noah, Nuu, *Naa tini hwey* (and others) along with his 7 family member were the sole survivors of a catastrophic flood aboard a floating craft landing on a tall mountain. To be honest, I believe we will soon confirm the Ark story through satellite imagery and when Turkey/Iran allow archeologists to excavate the believed site of what is believed the Ark. The final proof will be the DNA test of the materials they find.

In quick summary, Noah, his wife, their three sons and their wives landed on Ararat some 5,000 years ago, with provisions and animals of all kinds. Noah was 600 years old when they landed while his sons were a youthful 100 or so. Noah lived to the ripe old age of 950 and his sons lived nearly as long, seeing their great (times 8) grandchildren. Again, they were from an advanced civilization, though we know little of that (to date), and I am confident that we'll eventually prove that the pyramids and other ancient artifacts confirm this concept as well.

It's evidenced that Noah's sons understood the delicate art of *procreation* as they quickly began to create "nations" on the earth. Noah's eldest, Shem, remained close to home and became the father of the Israelite and Arab tribes (Semitics). Noah's middle son, Ham, migrated south and east throughout Africa and towards southern Asia, while Noah's youngest son, Japheth, remained around Turkey and then migrated north into Europe and northern Asia. Again, this history seems to coincide with the various mtDNA studies I've seen and other ancient histories discovered.

To me, one of the more amazing accounts that validate the accuracy of Jewish Scripture was concerning Noah's second son, Ham. As mentioned, *Ham* migrated south towards the African continent, and in his travels had a son who he named *Cush*, which translated means *"Black"*. Cush became the father of *Nimrod*, whose name means *rebellious/valiant*, which again validates this man who was recorded as being a *"mighty man in the earth"* (Gen 10:8-9, KJV). Considering our world of sports today, is there any doubt that many powerful and successful athletes are related to this mighty warrior, Nimrod? Let's see if mtDNA studies confirm this.

33

Now the histories of both *Israel* and *Isla*m come from the accounts of *Father Abraham*, the great (times 8) grandson of Noah. Abram (Exalted Father) grew-up in the Mesopotamia area (today's Iraq) and may have heard the Ark stories straight from Noah and/or Shem before God calls Abram to relocate to the Mediterranean coast. Abram follows God's direction and heads west to where the seafaring nomadic Philistines (his great Uncle's family) lived. It certainly doesn't take a scholar to discern that these nomad cousins of Abram's time are the ancestors of the Palestinians of today.

Abram travels around the area, going down the coast to Egypt and then back north to what today is Israel. At 80 years old, he's still fit, while his wife Sarai (Princess) remains childless well past the age of childbearing. During their travels, God changes Abram's name to Abraham or "Father of many", proclaiming that Abraham's family would be "as numerous as the stars" (Gen 26:4). Interestingly, Sarai has gone through menopause.

So, Sarai decides to control the situation by giving her hand-maid Hagar to Abraham as a concubine in order to have a son through her. Yet once Hagar conceives from Abraham, Sarai becomes jealous and mistreats Hagar, who in-turn runs away from the camp to the well at Shur where she is met by an angel of God, who says:

> *"Return to your mistress and submit to her authority". - "I will greatly multiply your descendants, so that they will be too numerous to count." - "You are now pregnant and will give birth to a son. You are to name him Ishmael (God hears), for the Lord has heard your cry of distress. This son of yours will be a wild man, as untamed as a wild donkey! He will raise his fist against everyone, and everyone will be against him. Yes, he will live in open hostility against all his relatives."* (Gen 16:9-12, NLT).

Hagar returns to Abraham's camp, humbles herself to Sarai, and raises Ishmael with his father Abraham. **Ishmael is considered the Father of Islam.** Thirteen years after the birth of Ishmael, God changes Sarai's name to Sarah (Queen) and tells Abraham and her that she will give birth to a son though she is now 90 years old. A year later and just after the destruction of Sodom and the nearby cities, Sarah indeed has Abraham's son, Isaac, who is the patriarch of the **Hebrews**. When Isaac was 36 years old, Sarah died, and, after a few years of mourning, Abraham then marries Keturah (Incense) who has 6 sons with Abraham that become the Midianites and various other Arab tribes of today.

As an added thought - Jesus (the Messiah) was also a descendent of Abraham through Israel's son, Judah, and "Christians" consider themselves as his children by adoption (Romans Chapter 8).

Again, just like Noah, there are unprecedented confirmations that Elohim (God) had His hand in every narrative from the earliest recorded times:

- Ishmael had <u>12</u> sons. (Islam)
- Isaac's son Jacob (renamed Israel) had <u>12</u> sons. (Jews)
- Jesus had <u>12</u> Disciples. (Christians)
- Keturah had <u>6</u> sons. (Arabs – A mix of Islam, Jew & Christian)
- <u>Over 50%</u> of the world's population considers Abraham their father through Ishmael, Isaac, the Arabic tribes and Christ

DNA studies and histories from the Jewish and other ancient writings confirm that we're just one, big, not-so-happy family that always yearns to better our cousins. Our colors, shapes, sizes and unique attributes were obviously inherited from Noah's sons and daughters-in-laws (of unknown parents) each having unique traits, like the dark traits of Cush's mom. As families grew and women demanded their own kitchen and closets, the environments they ended-up in also affected their physical traits. In essence, varying traits were certain to occur.

Though we all can likely claim to be children of Noah, it's also likely that Noah's three daughter's in-law had unique parent (who died in the flood). With that thought, I'm modestly confident that coming mtDNA (Maternal) studies will eventually trace our ancestry back to three unique sailor girls, while Paternal DNA will eventually trace us back to Noah.

So, all have descended from Noah. Interestingly, the pre-Abraham/Hindu Vedic God Indra is known as the Creator of all things, but particularly heaven, storms and flooding. This means that most religions today serve the same Creator. Though the Creators name is different, my research finds the common translation of all as "The One who Always Existed".

Here's another thought I'd like to leave you with:

-**Hinduism** reveals a God of creation, life and eternity
-**Judaism** reveals the timeline of man and the laws of God
-**Islam** reveals the judgement of God on those who forsake Him
-**Christianity** reveals the grace of God for those who seek Him

Chapter 9 – Indoctrination

All parents damage their children. It cannot be helped. Youth, like pristine glass, absorbs the prints of its handlers. Some parents smudge, others crack, a few shatter childhoods completely into jagged little pieces, beyond repair. Mitch Albom

Train up a child in the way he should go; even when he is old he will not depart from it. Prov 22:6, ESV

Blessed is the man who walks not in the counsel of the wicked, nor stands in the way of sinners, nor sits in the seat of scoffers; but his delight is in the law of the Lord, and on his law he meditates day and night. He is like a tree planted by streams of water that yields its fruit in its season, and its leaf does not wither. In all that he does, he prospers. Psalms 1:1-4, NET

~~~~~

If we are a global family, why are we so adversarial? As discussed earlier, a *Dark Side* most certainly exists, drawing people to it like a magnet. No matter how innocent someone may seem, all have selfish tendencies, and all that survived to 2 years-old have intentionally done wrong. My wife says selfishness is an obvious human trait since temper tantrums and selfishness never need to be taught, while they must be taught to share.

As such, either our nature is evil or some kind-of external force (Adversary) is playing against the *Creator's* "creators". Obviously, I believe it's a combination of both, and as Alinsky suggested, the ancient adversary is *Lucifer* who hates those created in the Creator's image (mankind). As is depicted in the Star Wars sagas, this *Dark Side* seems to have a targeted focus against balancing The Force with the family being the key target. I won't spoil the latest Star Wars movie, but I must admit the episode, ***Rise of Skywalker*** *(J. J. Abrams/Walt Disney)* is now one of my favorites in the saga and validates this concept.

Now any commonsense individual would admit that all families are dysfunctional. When any two unique people come together for any reason (especially marriage), it's not long before personalities, beliefs, dreams and concepts collide into confusion, disagreement and dysfunction. I'm confident that no two people who have ever lived would agree on every issue. That said, I don't believe they are meant to since *"two heads are usually better than one"*. Likewise, two eyes give a better perspective (view) than one allowing for field of depth and enhanced perception. We used to call our two-man kayak a marriage counseling devise since it quickly revealed how couples worked together and synchronize their strengths. Our differences cause chaos and dysfunction at times, but it also creates *dynamic power*!

Now there are family units that are beyond dysfunctional and would be considered dangerous. Sadly, we see these in the news almost daily. Dangerous families seldom create much more than despair, and it can always relate back to selfish intent and ambition. Yet even from such a family as this, a champion can (and often does) arise. Sometimes the most desperate situations give rise to the greatest opportunities and results.

So, we all have a combination of attributes passed down from our parents and their parents before them. Though the physical is mostly unalterable, we do have the opportunity to choose and alter our spiritual, psychological and purposeful characteristics. That said, we often carry emotional challenges attained from our youth no matter how much we may fight it.

Within every family tree there resides the blood of slave and king, harlot and hero - ours is to choose which limb to climb out on!

Of course, there are other communities beyond our own family such as friends, neighbors, classmates, church groups and even worldwide communities from internet and news venues. Each of these communities are comprised of unique, challenged and imperfect human beings just like us, so it's reasonable to assume that we could find ourselves in potentially dangerous, dysfunctional or dynamic relationships that shift the course of our life and actions! *Indoctrination* is therefore a reality, with the most pliable target being the young.

In our family, we've certainly tried to influence our children and grandchildren with the ideals of honoring others, being responsible and having hope for the future, while encouraging individualism. Above all we've tried to instill the concept of trusting Providence (the Force). Sure, we've had and will have our shortcomings, but even our weaknesses can be a lesson for their benefit. Failures have given us a chance to grow with our children, grandchildren and hopefully our great grandchildren to come. We didn't know it all when we started, and to be honest, as time has progressed, we've only grown in the realization that we are even more clueless than we thought. Teaching our family (or letting them see) that we are imperfect humans, provides them with the confidence and grace to accept their own failures along with their successes and to press-on though often added humility.

Our youngest was the only son that we pushed to join the Boy Scouts of America (BSA). The BSA oath defines what I believe is the ideal doctrine for any child: *"On my honor I will do my best to do my duty to God and my country and to obey the Scout Law; to help other people at all times; to keep myself physically strong, mentally awake, and morally straight"*. Similarly, the Scout Law reads - *"A Scout is Trustworthy, Loyal, Helpful, Friendly, Courteous, Kind, Obedient, Cheerful, Thrifty, Brave, Clean, and Reverent"*. Yep, perfect attributes for any child, and when confirmed at every meeting through the Oath, *"Always be prepared"*, these foundational standards are above reproach.

The best aspect of scouting was the organization's way to incorporate the parents into meetings and adventures. I can honestly say that I was standing on the shoulders of giants who lead our troops and who exemplified the Oath, Law and Motto each week and during outings. Their example helped me to understand much and helped my son achieve his Eagle Scout on the BSA's 100th Anniversary at the age of 13. This community of imperfect people worked together to achieve something that continues to amaze me. Were there other "not-so-honorable" leaders? Absolutely, but these had little influence within our troop or upon our son. Overall, an amazing bunch of heroes!

Sadly, few children have quality role models like our Scout leaders. Most American youth are being indoctrinated by programs like *The Simpsons* and other programs where the same paradigm of a bumbling father, clueless mother and all-wise child (reflecting the viewer) promotes lying and manipulation. My son revealed a similar theme in recent Disney-style movies, where a young intelligent, energetic and often misfit girl uses an old bungling or weak male to help her conquer a crumbling or apathetic world. These plots aren't just a fun pun to excite our youth, but a means to brainwash the inquisitive and vulnerable to distrust and fight their parents. Is it any wonder that so many selfish, dependent and unstable younger adults still live at home, play video games and watch programs like the Simpsons? The enemy is obviously at work using media and our education system.

When a family lacks a father figure through birth outside of marriage, divorce, death or a crazy work schedule, the young (male and female) will seek another father figure to revere. And it's usually one with a dangerous spirit. In most instances it doesn't turn out well, and the wandering youth ends-up in the clutches of the *Dark Side* as easy prey.

Mistrusting and challenging authority is the common result of a fatherless family, and these manipulated children become a manipulative hand themselves. One thing that all children pick-up on is *hypocrisy!*

Adolf Hitler and the Nazi Party understood that an indoctrinated youth would be the power of the future. His infamous Hitler Jugend (Youth) program eventually became compulsory for all children, ages 10-18, with special teachings for the "Little Fellows" (ages 6–10). Being part of a proud and powerful group with uniforms and team armbands, "Mein Kompf" was shoveled into their minds while children give the Nazi salute to teachers as a sign of allegiance to the Fuhrer. Those unenthused by the cause were "retrained" in Nazi ideals or punished. Membership in the National Socialist Teachers League was a must as evidenced by a 97% membership rate. To ensure a fully controlled populace, Hitler's greatest tactic was to employ both parents away from home, forcing the young into schools that enveloped them into the Third Reich.

With the United States embracing industry after World War II, the women who worked for the war cause became comfortable with the added income that their trade gave the family. As such, many exchanged their priority of raising future generations for the potential of added income. They relinquished their children to indoctrination within the U. S. Public Education System, believing that the systems and teachers had the best interest at heart for their child. The loss of the "mother at home" has been one of the greatest tragedies in our nation's history. At a recent American Federation of Teachers (AFT) conference, the Union President Randi Weingarten said, "Our democracy is under assault," as she went on to attack President Trump and his supporters. She then said "Teachers have always had power. We need to own our power", and "we need to build our power so we can move our agenda…".

In 1962, the U. S. Supreme Court ruled to remove *Religion* (family faith) from our public education system with a nearly unanimous vote. Though they couldn't force students to deny their religion, pray or read their Bibles, they could limit and eventually ban outward acts supporting such. Many congressional and judicial members, along with various organizations like the American Civil Liberties Union (ACLU), Freedom from Religion Foundation (FFRF) and Southern Poverty Law Center (SPLC) have sued schools and individuals for any stance that resembles a citizen's First Amendment rights (almost always Christian).

After removing God from our schools in 1962, it was a simple matter for that same basic Supreme Court in 1973 to deny the *2nd Cornerstone of Life* for millions of future Americans by promoting and funding the murder of the unborn child in the mother's womb. Leveraging an unpopular war and a call for free love, *Alinsky's* rules were powerfully implemented to control the minds and hearts of the American people through the media and educationally elite, setting a precedence that tore our nation in half. With *Roe v Wade*, our nation has enacted the greatest holocaust in the history of the world (except the global flood), killing nearly 100 million unborn Americans since 1973.

Let's finish with some sad U. S. stats from a few recent Pew Research Polls and World Population Review summaries:

- 25% of parents are unmarried
- 15% of 25 to 35-year-olds Americans still live at home
- The U. S. ranks 24th globally in Math, Reading and Science
- Single Parent Home have significantly increased since the 1970's:
        51% Black, 27% Hispanic, 17% White, 10% Asian

I'll share more pointed statistics in the coming chapters, but let these sink in. For those that believe we humans are evolving, I'd like to hear your theory on how any of this is an improvement or revelation of evolutionary progress. In all honesty, there is an indoctrination happening around the world, and we must open our eyes to the threat being made against humanity. Hitler and Stalin are mild compared to the evils being perpetrated on the unborn, our youth and today's families.

Chapter 10 –Gold & Rules

While the people are virtuous they cannot be subdued; but when once they lose their virtue, they will be ready to surrender their liberties to the first external or internal invader. Samuel Adams

But a Constitution of Government once changed from Freedom, can never be restored. Liberty once lost is lost forever. When the People once surrender their share in the Legislature, and their Right of defending the Limitations upon the Government, and of resisting every Encroachment upon them, they can never regain it. President John Adams

*For the love of money is the root of all kinds of evil.*1 Tim 6:10, NLT

~~~~~

Our nation's founders committed their very lives and fortunes to remove the chains of England's tyranny over the American colonies, to establish a *"people's government, made for the people, made by the people, and answerable to the people"* - Daniel Webster. Men and women who'd struggled against an overpowering government body of elites and were willing to overcome the tyranny and establishing a nation of free people that could boldly stand side-by-side with their fellow Americans on the Cornerstones of this new nation.

Even so, our founders understood the weaknesses and selfish hearts of men having seen the failure of Democracies around the globe. Because of this understanding, they decided to establish a Republic (*Public Entity)* form of government that divided the power and control of our nation into three equal and yet unique Branches. Each Branch with specific areas of oversight and the ability to keep one another in check by a set of laws and rules that would be difficult to bend or alter yet easy to follow. (See *Constitution, Bill of Rights, Amendments and Laws)*

The three branches of government established were the **Executive** (Presidential), **Judicial** (Courts) and **Legislative** (laws & finance). To ensure that the Legislative powers of government remain in the hands of the people while still supporting the independent States (avoiding a Democracy), they split the Legislative powers into two Houses:

- The House of Representatives (Lower House) comprised of an individual representing local districts within the state, and

- The Senate (Upper House) comprised of two representatives from each state.

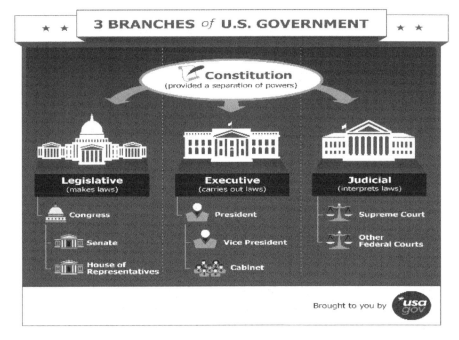

The 3 Branches of the U. S. Government

* Appendix II provides Congressional balance of power during each Administration along with a current profile of our *Senators* and a summary of our *Representatives*. I'd suggest you look closely at each.

Our basic form of government was designed for our Federal (national) powers and suggested for adoption under Article 10 of our Constitution for the States. This allows for a common *rule of law* across the expanding United States, specifically establishing a Republican form of government throughout. Yet, even as our founders were defining this unique Republic, there were many who desired power and wealth more than the justice for all, challenging our governing principles. Thank God for George Washington and the other leaders who remained strong during such adverse times. Sadly, the principle of *"He who has the gold makes the rules while he who makes the rules takes the gold"* was a problem even then.

In 1929, the Permanent Apportionment Act set the maximum number of House Representatives to 435 members, determined by the population (Census Data) taken every 10 years. Some states have 1 Representative while other states have more Representatives and obviously more power during the various votes. This variance is a continual challenge in passing bills. For example, when Alaska (1 Representative) votes in opposition to California (55 Representatives), it's obvious who has the power even though Alaska is over 4 times the size of California. This is where the Senate come in to play as each State has an equal tow (2) Senators that represent their State's interests in a final vote.

Another challenge addressed in our nation's early years was the election of a President. To avoid a "Popular Vote", *Virginia* proposed that members of the *House of Representatives* should elect the President since they directly represent the people. James Wilson of Pennsylvania (yep, a possible relative) took the thought a bit deeper by proposing a further *Separation of Powers* between the *Executive* and *Congressional Branches* with each State choosing *"Electors"* (non-Congressmen) to represent the people in electing the President and Vice President. This would ensure that no Legislator would be beholden to a potential President or vice versa. Absolute genius!

Article II, Section 1 of the Constitution outlines how the Electoral process is to work. Each state's Electors are equal to their Senate and House members. Currently there are 100 Senators and 435 Representatives combined, while in 1961 the 23rd Amendment provided the District of Columbia (D. C.) with 3 Electors as well creating a combined Electoral College of 538 Electors. Alexander Hamilton outlined the intent of this concept suggesting that *"A small number of persons, selected by their fellow citizens from the general mass, will be most likely to possess the information and discernment requisite to such complicated [tasks]"*.

For Electoral College votes however, population does matter, and it matters significantly. Using Alaska and California again, Alaska has 3 Electoral votes while California has 57. If we had just the two states, California could determine the Presidency every election. California has 57 of the 538 Electoral votes (over 10% of our national power) in electing the President and Vice President with only 4.3% of our nation's land mass. On top of that, each State determines how it will assign the Electoral votes - all to one candidate or apportioned out.

California is also a great example for voter manipulation. With tens of millions of illegal and non-U.S. citizens residing in California, illegally including them in National Census effects our *Representative Districts* and *Electoral College,* delegitimizing our Congressional balance and Presidency. Obviously, these unlawful voters would help to create laws that benefit non-citizens at the expense of the Americans. Eventually, we the citizens would become the minority and an illegal populace will control our nation, voting for whoever promises them the most from the taxpayer monies. This is the Democratic Party plan.

As of this writing, the U. S. Supreme Court is considering the sovereignty of the Electors at the State level. Due to State-unique definitions, confusion and uncertainty, there are numerous states challenging our Electoral system in several ways. California and other wholly Democrat states intend to seriously jeopardize an honest election. This is a huge issue, and I hope the Justices interpret our Founder's concepts appropriately!

> *"The American Republic will endure until the day Congress discovers that it can bribe the public with the public's money."* Tocqueville.

Yes, *We the People* must awaken from our complacency and take our responsibilities seriously. Our vote is critical. The fabric of America has not just worn thin in spots but is literally ripping apart at some critical seams that hold our Constitution together. There is an existing and eminent threat against our nation's Cornerstones and her Republic.

> *"What is the most sacred duty and the greatest source of our security in a Republic? An inviolable respect for the Constitution and Laws."* Alexander Hamilton.

The recent Impeachment of President Trump by the Democratic House, though rejected by the Senate, has sadly set a new precedence for impeaching a sitting President whenever an opposition majority resides in the House. This has established a new set of rules that undermines the strengths of our nation's laws and our combined statehood. It has not only revealed the divide within our nation but has potentially driven a permanent wedge between her people. This latest attempt to unseat President Trump was more of an attempted *coup d'état* much like the April 12, 1861 Confederate attack on Fort Sumter.

Chapter 11 – Slavery

God who gave us life gave us liberty. And can the liberties of a nation be thought secure when we have removed their only firm basis, a conviction in the minds of the people that these liberties are of the Gift of God? That they are not to be violated but with His wrath? Indeed, I tremble for my country when I reflect that God is just, that His justice cannot sleep forever. Thomas Jefferson

God created humankind in his own image, in the image of God he created them, male and female he created them. Genesis 1:27, NET

There is no longer Jew or Gentile, slave or free, male and female. For you are all one in Christ Jesus. Gal 3:28, NLT

~~~~~

Let's take a historic look at the world as it was during the time of the Pilgrims and other Colonist when they came to the *New World* and created the nation we have today. Our focus will certainly be on *slavery* but also on the thoughts of man throughout.

After the nomadic Asians came to the west, Icelanders claim that Leif Erikson (around 1,000 AD) was the first to discover the Americas (which is likely true). Yet it was Christopher Columbus who became the first trader/explorer to establish a sailing route to the Americas in the 1400's. As history suggests, Columbus left Spain with the intent to find a westward route to the wealthy India, which is evidenced by his naming the Bermudian natives, "Indios" (Spanish for Indian). After his 4 mostly successful voyages to the new land, the race was on for the Europeans to conquer this new world.

Spain and Portugal became the primary invaders/conquerors of the islands and southern Americas while England and France focused on the Northern American continent. After establishing settlements in Jamestown (Virginia) and Plymouth (Mass), colonizing the new world and taking advantage of the fertile land and natural resources called to all that where were oppressed or stymied by the tyranny in the old world of Europe. Most would come for opportunity, some for adventure and exploration, while nearly all came to escape the British persecution.

Coming to the new world was seldom easy. Finding a ship and paying unprecedented fairs for passage was difficult with many being swindled of their finances on deceitful promises. Of those who would find passage, many would die in transit, and many others would die shortly after landing on the new shores due to harsh weather, lack of provisions and basic uncertainty. But opportunity certainly called. Here's a basic scenario that would play in the new world's economy and politics:

The Southern States - leaned towards agriculture for their success, necessitating large expanses of land and tough sun baked laborers. As industry and power grew in the North, the battle to remain relevant and have equal pull within government necessitated the South to expand and increase productivity. Laborers, land (often possessed by native Americans) and shipping were essential to the survival and success of the South.

The Northern States – with harsh land and seasons, leaned towards mining, manufacturing and industry for their success. With the abundance of mineral resources and a growing global market, the Industrial Revolution created wealthy business owners, investors and bankers that naturally began to control the governing body of America.

According to historical documents, before 1655 there were no legal slaves in the American colonies, only *indentured servants* (term slaves). This has been a common practice throughout history and was such during our earliest years. Early on, most indentured servants were white Europeans from Ireland, Wales and northern Europe. Men and their families who couldn't afford passage to the Americas would "rent" their own lives out for a time (usually 7 years) in order to pursue their hopes of a better life. Though seeming inhumane, an indentured servant was an honorable means of hope and freedom for those who otherwise could not afford the price of opportunity and escape from tyranny.

Here's a quick thought – Those who paid for passage to the new land would often spend all they had only to find themselves alone and in competition with others in their new world. Not only was the transit hard and sometimes deadly but establishing a home and means of income was an extreme challenge to every newcomer and new competitor.

An indentured servant though was considered a commodity and immediately received their basic needs to survive and work. Once ashore, such servants were generally provided room and board, kept healthy, and taught a skill or trade in order to gain the greatest return on investment. During their indenture, such servants would learn the lingo, the lay of the land, and build a reputation that would precede their release, giving them an instant platform on which to build a future.

In the early years of America's colonization, there were more white indentured servants than black. In time though, as plantations opened-up for Britain and the Colonies in the south for cotton, sugar and other highly sought-after commodities, it was necessary to find servants who were more capable of hard work in the hot sun. The best and cheapest commodity for indenture were Africans captured by opposing African tribes and shipped to the Americas for just such a purpose. Initially, these slaves sold by their cousins would be *Indentured Servants* just like their European cousins.

Interestingly, Anthony Johnson, a Negro from what is today's Angola, was an *indentured servant* working on a tobacco farm in 1619. After release from service, Johnson himself became a successful farmer in this "land of opportunity". In 1654 though, Johnson had his own *indentured servant* named John Casor who supposedly escaped from Johnson (during or after his term, I'm unsure). Casor found a job working for a white man named Robert Parker. Discovering that Casor was working for Parker, Johnson sued Parker in the Northampton Court in 1655 with the court ruling to not only return Casor to Johnson but that he would remain the property of Johnson as an indefinite slave. This order by a single judge opened the floodgates for slavery throughout the new world, and within 16 years, it was fully legal throughout the British Empire to own a slave for life.

In 1830, there were 3,775 black families living in the South who owned black slaves. By 1860 (just 30 years later), the city of New Orleans alone had over 3,000 slaves owned by black households.

A century after the courts permitted slavery within the colonies, our Founding Fathers themselves officially declaring slavery immoral with our *Declaration of Independence* stating: ***"We hold these truths to be self-evident, that all men are created equal, that they are endowed by their Creator with certain unalienable Rights, that among these are Life, Liberty and the pursuit of Happiness."*** It's a tragedy that those who opposed the concept of slavery did so in the quiet of their own homes while those who leveraged slavery for their own purposes and success became a powerful voice in commerce and politics.

As suggested, the Southern States depended on land and labor. As America was expanding in territories and global power, the states were also jockeying for power with the Southern states needing land and cheap labor to work it. To attain land, migrations west necessitated taking land from the indigenous peoples (Indians), and to do so required the Indians to be sequestered on specific lands called Reservations, lands that were often woefully inadequate for their sustainment. Over time, these peoples would become almost wholly dependent (enslaved) on the government to survive while being shunned from participating in the American dream and her opportunities.

America's 7th President (Andrew Jackson) was our nation's first **Democratic** President. This aggressively Southern, pro-slavery President was also the catalyst for the government's sequestering of our Native American tribes onto government defined reservations. Instead of honorably including these original American citizens into the new nation, he feared these peoples and considered them *enemies of the state* and their lands as being *conquered territory*. Unfortunately for the Native Americans and future slaves, Jackson handily defeating the anti-slavery **Republican** John Quincy Adams with over 60% of the Electoral vote.

From these perspectives, the **Republican** and **Democrat** parties evolved. Of course, there are many, many facets to every concept, but the bottom line can always be attributed to **commerce** and **control**.

The **Democratic Party** of Andrew Jackson was designed as a political power in support of the South's agricultural realm. Plantations required land and laborers. The party platform challenged the "corrupt aristocracy" (wealthy business owners) of the North who were growing in strength from the wealth gained through industry and invention. The South promoted state sovereignty over federal control hoping to expand their plantations throughout the south and west.

The **Republican Party** of John Quincy Adams and Abraham Lincoln was a response to limit Jackson's plan for expanded slavery and control of lands throughout the new nation. The Grand Old Party (GOP) was comprised of the successful business, banking and industrial entities of the North and feared the South's expansion and vote (Electoral power). The North also depended on commodities from the South and were concerned with their potential separation from the Union.

Unable to overcome their selfish desires for commerce and control, leadership within both parties were willing to divide the people of this Land of Liberty and compel them into a war against their brother. Again, the greed for power and control always corrupt. The result was a divided and devastated United States, and an unprepared nation for millions of emancipated slaves. Having no plan or path on how to integrate these new citizens into society, these uneducated and poor slaves were destined to return to the Plantation as inadequately paid servant employees.

With the horrors of the *Trail of Tears*, the sanctioned abuses and killings of American natives and slaves, and a complacent populace, is it any wonder that America's sovereignty was challenged by our great Civil War? 100 years after declaring *Independence for all* her citizenry, the *God of nature* would require the blood of our nation's strongest for the atrocities against their fellow man. Nearly ½ of our American losses from all American wars and battles since our Independence came from American fighting American.

Though freed in the eyes of the law, the newly emancipated slaves remained chained by personal self-doubt and prejudices of their surroundings. As inventions such as the Cotton Gin and tractor came along, these uneducated laborers sought work elsewhere, migrating to areas where uneducated labor was needed. Battling the prejudices of color, these Americans found themselves in "urban plantations" with limited prospects for expanding their education and opportunities.

Mind you, success and failure are not a race, color or other trait issue, but always a heart issue. Here's a simple concept I'll cover in more detail later that may help to simplify your life's choices, and that I espouse in my previous book, ***A.S.K. for Purpose***.

The "H.O.P.E. Rose" © 2018,

Though unknown to most, the ***H.O.P.E. Rose*** has been the guide for all human successes throughout history. As a Navy SEAL, it's only natural to define a strategic and moral compass for my actions, though I can assure you, life still has its challenges, even with such a great tool.

I share this concept here as an example of how men and women throughout history have overcome times of great challenge and hardship and difficulty to become champions, no matter what their color, race or creed. People like George Washington Carver, Booker T. Washington and Frederick Douglas undoubtably followed the *H.O.P.E. Rose* out of slavery and on to success. Let's look at the Compass Points:

Honor - *True North*! Being moral and ethical in thought and action allows Providence to work on your behalf. Honorable intent establishes confidence and the resolve to act even in times of uncertainty.

Opportunity – Keeping our senses tuned to our surroundings is essential for both obstacles and opportunities. As Providence works on your behalf, manning the crows-nest with spyglass at hand is essential.

Purpose – Our greatest treasure and objective in life, where passions and talents merge and a desire for leaving a legacy are fulfilled.

Enthusiasm – Pursuing Purpose, capitalizing on Opportunities and knowing all is with Honorable intent creates enthusiasm and power.

The **F.E.A.R.** points are "guides" that keep us on course. **Fright, Emotion**, **Animosity** and **Regret** help us stay on course.

There's another compass that was revealed in *Disney's* blockbuster film series *Pirates of the Caribbean*. Jack Sparrow's *magic compass* points to "what you want most" – I call it the "*Desire Compass*). In essence, the arrow points towards your *desire*, but if you lacked a firm *desire*, the compass would either swing wildly or lock-up. An amazing life-truth! *Without Purpose there's confusion!*

Sadly, after hundreds of years of slavery (continuing to today), few in America have found either Compass (*H.O.P.E. or Desire*), and therefore, many of our greatest minds and talents have remained in the chains of slavery, to those who would use them for their own *power and profit*. My hope is to change this evil through this book by presenting to you some hidden truths by helping to reveal your heart's *Desire* and providing a map to a better future for you and our nation using *Honor, Opportunity, Purpose and Enthusiasm* while being held in check using the *F.E.A.R.* aspects as we press forward.

Chapter 12 – Rights & Responsibilities

Within every family tree exists slave and king, harlot and hero – yet it is our choice of the limb we climb out on. Daniel Wilson

All the miseries and evils which men suffer from vice, crime, ambition, injustice, oppression, slavery and war, proceed from their despising or neglecting the precepts contained in the Bible. Noah Webster

For freedom Christ has set us free; stand firm therefore, and do not submit again to a yoke of slavery. Galatians 5:1, ESV

~~~~~

In the gospels of *Matthew (25:14-30)* Jesus shares the *Parable of the Talents*, which I'd suggest you read, but let me summarize it:

The parable is about three servants who were each given *talents* (money) which they were to use/invest until their master's return. At his return, two of the servants revealed that their *talents* had doubled to which he commended the servants and rewarded them commensurate to their return on investment (ROI). The third servant didn't trust the master and hid his *talent*, so when the Master returned and asked for an account of his actions, he presented his talent back without increase. The master then took the *talent* from the third servant and gave it to the other calling the third servant *"wicked and slothful"*. He then had him cast into *"outer darkness"*. Truly a hard concept that challenged me for years but now makes sense!

The term *talent* at the time of Christ was somewhat ambiguous, but it generally reflected a person's *lifetime salary* based on their vocation or *skills*, establishing a net-worth for their work. Our English term *talent* is founded on this term and principle. When we say someone has talent, it means they have value in their ability and skill worthy of a return. In summary, using your abilities, skills and talents to enrich, honor and serve others is what brings return. As presented by Jesus, those who don't use their talents to enrich, honor or serve others are considered wicked and slothful, eventually losing all.

In Luke's Gospel (19:11-27), he shares a slightly different version of this parable, suggesting that the Master not only gave financial blessings to the good servants but puts them in charge of cities. Here's another concept that I believe Jesus was explaining: that the servants (all of us) are not only rewarded for wise investing but rewarded even more for freely giving the **gain** back to the *Master*! As such, the Master was not only honored but had proof he could trust the servant.

Faithfulness returns opportunity.

Here's an added truth from the *Parable of the Talents*: Since the evil servant hid his talent out of distrust of the master, he obviously needed to beg, rob or exploit to survive. His lack of respect for the Master and selfishness towards his fellowman were a dishonor causing him to take without giving and the eventually lose his very soul.

Without Purpose there's Perversion.

The Apostle Paul says it this way:

> *The acts of the flesh are obvious: sexual immorality, impurity and debauchery; idolatry and witchcraft; hatred, discord, jealousy, fits of rage, selfish ambition, dissensions, factions and envy; drunkenness, orgies, and the like. I warn you, as I did before, that those who live like this will not inherit the kingdom of God.* (5 Gal 19-21, NIV)

Going out on a limb, I'd propose that each of Paul's noted *acts of the flesh* are a symptom of a life without *Purpose* and living with *hidden talent*. Instead of using the *Desire compass* in respect to the *H.O.P.E. Rose*, a selfish man will allow the *F.E.A.R.* points to guide his actions and allow guilt to open the door to slavery of the flesh and a weakening of the spirit. Like cancer, bad cells feed off good cells, corrupting them and their purpose and spreading throughout the body.

After the *Industrial Revolution* as American prosperity was spreading across the nation and globe, America and most western nations fell prey to selfish acts resulting from this prosperity. *The Roaring 1920's* revealed an America that flaunted her success without monitoring her *H.O.P.E.* and *F.E.A.R.* compass points. By the late 20's bad investments and dealings with other nations sent the world into a *Great Depression* and our *Second World War*. I must caveat this though that it wasn't the success which caused the calamities for America but the greed and arrogance of many in leadership. It wasn't President Hoover that caused the global crisis leading to the War but an elite few who strategically planned a global crisis in order to capture national and global power.

Sadly, America today is living upon a similarly shaky foundation of unsound prosperity built upon a one-dimensional facade of glitz and glamor controlled by Hedge Fund investors, the media, our Hollywood elite and sports heroes. Mind you, pursuit of happiness is an absolute privilege of having the other Cornerstones solidly in place, but without honor, abundance leads to apathy which in-turn leads to what Paul calls the *acts of the flesh*. When people no longer honor the *Master* or one another, the talents they've been given will be unused and taken away and their being cast into *outer darkness*.

A good example of our depravity was the *Super Bowl LVI Halftime show* with Jennifer Lopez portraying a pole dancer in an X-rated movie while dozens of beautiful and innocent girls dressed in white were depicted in cages. It's amazing that women viciously attack men for being perverts when these same women proclaim this event as "empowering". Mind you, I am wholly male and have spent my entire life internally fighting sexual fantasies as women flaunt their wares at every turn (especially at Naval bases). These women then complain when men try to take them up on their offer. **It's a trap!**

Each of these girls and women (Lopez included) have been used as sex-slaves for the minds of men who lack a battle to fight and a beauty to rescue. Why are we so enamored with sports in America and around the globe? Because we lack the challenge of pursuit in our own lives. Many men, designed on testosterone and desire, sit in front of a television set and yell at the refs watching other men compete. Such men are easy prey to those who make $millions on their testosterone filled fantasies.

Our *RIGHTS* endowed by our Creator give us life, liberty and the ability to pursue happiness. Our *RESPONSIBILITIES* require us to use these *Rights* to honor the Master, our fellow man, and the planet we have been given. There are two basic reasons that men (and women) fail to pursue their purpose or invest their talent:

The Temptation of Abundance - When abundance is available and pursuit is unnecessary, it's human nature to fall prey to *the acts of the flesh*. King David was a perfect example of this. While his warriors were defending their nation, David was safe in his castle until Bathsheba decided to take a bath just below his window. Not in the pursuit, he was enticed, acted on his fleshly impulse, and even killed Bathsheba's husband to cover it up. Abundance without pursuit is a sure way to failure.

The Temptation of Slavery – It may sound contrary to our present world view, but slavery is an accepted state. The Africans captured by their fellow Africans should have fought to the end giving their all for freedom and families, but they didn't. The servants that first came to

America should have fought against slavery from the very start, never allowing another to chain, abuse or rule over them, but they didn't. Instead, they became complacent on the *Plantation* allowing the master to control their lives, their families and their future. We have millions of Americans today who still live on the *Plantation* being controlled by someone else of their own free-will. Mind you, these are not blacks alone but anyone who allows another to control their lives. Like the testosterone driven men who spend their fortunes on sports and sexual fantasies, we have an entire nation of slaves being manipulated by the wealthy "plantation owners".

Let's look again at the concepts of *Indentured Servants* and *Slaves* specific to our nation's history and her future. The *Indentured Servant* is an individual willing to contract his/her service for a given period and a potential future opportunity. The *Slave,* however, is either taken against his will or sells himself for an indefinite time without a compensatory future opportunity. Slavery is transferred from generation to generation in the flesh and in the mind and requires an individual revolution.

Though not the *Master*, there are those within the *Plantation* whose role is like the slave foremen of old. One of the "family" who is hired to manipulate their brothers to keep them on the plantation. We see this today in people like Jesse Jackson, Al Sharpton, Maxine Watters, and so many others who have become millionaires by keeping the *Plantation* in operation and the deception hidden behind a smile and flashy lifestyle. We also see it through individuals and institutions like Zuckerberg, Planned Parenthood, various preachers, Sports and News Casters and many cult leaders. Cigarette companies, drug manufacturers, movie producers, sports team owners, and so many more ensnare (enslave) others for their personal gain.

Free porn websites aren't an intent to share art, and free drugs aren't an intent to open the mind of others. Each are a tactic to enslave and prosper within an abundant society without purpose. People without purpose have been and always will be the target for the Plantation owner. Lopez wasn't sharing her art; she was being used to entice millions of viewers into the world of sexual fantasies through media. While she grabbed her barely covered crotch before millions of children, the *National Human Trafficking Hotline* was hard pressed to help the more than 23,000 estimated U. S. annual victims of abuse, 65 percent of whom were women. Around the globe the numbers are even more staggering with an estimated 25 million people being held captive, abused or manipulated by human traffickers.

One of the most amazing enslavements is in the arsenal of our politicians: the chains of guilt. Leveraging the compassion of the masses, politicians incite the *guilt factor* in order to control the minds, actions and monies of those who know they haven't earned their foundations through purpose and pursuit. The honest and caring are manipulated into fighting for the lost, downtrodden and weak but not in a way that is good for either the victim or the hero.

The "Robin Hood" concept is noble when a tyrannical government enslaves its people. Fighting for freedom and others is normally a righteous act. Yet our wealthiest and most glamorous elite (actors, athletes and politicians) incite hatred against others who strive for success through business and pursuit. The wealthy and elite guilt *We the People* for the oppressions of others and for a failing world while they themselves have plush houses and fly around on private jets.

It's not about rescuing the downtrodden. It's about creating a slave populace that funds their propaganda while advancing their slave tactics. Why would any nation promote a select group unless it intends to enslave? Such are the actions of instituting a Black History Month and Gay Pride Month. Promoting any group over another always intends to divide and enslave. Many who desire to be compassionate are simply manipulated by those seeking control. ***Without purpose, perversion. Without investment, enslavement.***

I'd recommend reading the 2020 DNC Platform (on-line in PDF format). On the surface it sounds very compassionate, while it's entirely about enslavement and control. The Party's goal is to take the burden of responsibility from all in order to give control to the elite few within government. The party intent is to divide, pervert and enslave by destroying our nation's Cornerstones. It's not a platform of compassion but control! Here's their bottom line:

1. Government control of all programs (Socialism vice Republic)
2. Government take-over of corporations (Steal the Gold)
3. Equality for everyone (Enslavement)
4. Murder of the unborn American (Killing the Creation)
5. Promoting sexual perversion (Destroy the Soul)

Jesus said it best, *"The thief comes only to steal and kill and destroy; I have come that they may have life and have it to the full."* (Matt 10:10, NIV).

Chapter 13 – Slavery Today

We are called the nation of inventors. And we are. We could still claim that title and wear its loftiest honors if we had stopped with the first thing we ever invented, which was human liberty. Mark Twain

Since the general civilization of mankind, I believe there are more instances of the abridgment of the freedom of the people by gradual and silent encroachments of those in power than by violent and sudden usurpations. James Madison

For I know the plans I have for you, declares the LORD, plans to prosper you and not to harm you, plans to give you hope and a future. Jeremiah 29:11, NIV

~~~~~

The compasses of *Desire* and *H.O.P.E.* are man's only means to unlock the chains that bind him. Both require *ACTION*. Having a direction and intent is only good if you're willing to pursue and change. Success always necessitates *ACTION*.

Before our Founders signed the Declaration of Independence, Alexander Fraser Tytler, a Professor of Universal History at the University of Edinburgh, Scotland, defined what he termed, *The Cycle of Democracy,* stating:

> *"The average of the world's great civilizations before they decline has been 200 years. These nations have progressed in this sequence: From* **bondage** *to spiritual faith; from* **faith** *to great* **courage***; from courage to* **liberty***; from liberty to* **abundance***; from abundance to* **selfishness***; from selfishness to* **complacency***; from complacency to* **apathy***; from apathy to* **dependency***; from dependency back again to* **bondage***"*.

I'd like to propose that nearly every nation in history has gone through Tytler's Cycle in one way or another. Even the African tribes from where most American slaves had come were the likely result of such a Cycle with tribes that had become complacent and apathetic finding themselves in bondage and on their way to the Colonies.

The United States of America has surpassed the 200-year mark but not without our Civil War and other major actions delaying our retreat into bondage. Yet as we look at the cycle it's easy to see that we've come from *abundance* through *selfishness* and have adopted a *complacent* and *apathetic* attitude. Considering our *Socialist leaning* presidential candidates for our 2020 election, I'd propose we are now teetering on the verge of jumping headlong into dependency and bondage. Thankfully, the *Wild Card* seems to be reshuffling the deck and challenging the players at the table forcing most Americans to be courageous and fight for liberty. Let's see how this has come to pass as we attempt to remain *One Nation Under God*.

While George Washington received 100% of the Electoral vote during both of his terms, factions had started on day-one about how our government would be designed. Little has changed since Thomas Jefferson and John Adams were at odds, though the political landscape became more visible some 50 years later with the divide between John Quincy Adams (Republican) and General Andrew Jackson (Democrat) over who would control the country, her people and their finances. Follow the money and control!

As the **Board of Directors**, *We the People* must seek the truth instead of allowing ourselves to be carried along with the current of apathy into the hype of partisan politics. Political factions are not like dedication to a football team where we wear the jerseys or don the hats. No, this is a critical decision that will determine the future of our families, our States, our Nation and the world! As mentioned earlier, it's my belief that God has established the United States of America as a *City on a Hill* (envisioned by John Winthrop in 1610), reflecting freedom and honor to the world. If we lose that purpose, we will certainly become little more than a byword in history. Obviously, we are failing in our call and floating lazily through Tytler's Cycle of Democracy nearly to the point of slipping over the cliff.

The reason we can relate to each of these stages within our nation today is because we have a split people and not necessarily between Democrat and Republican. In this instance, we are a nation split in every faction possible because of media hype and greedy leaders. We're split men against women, black/white/brown/other colors, rich against poor, scientist against religious, state against state, college against college, religion against religion and even by sports teams and media venues. As suggested, we are still battling our Civil War, with politicians and external powers wholeheartedly promoting the battle (divisions) in order to control our populace and our purse. Like any competition (such as sports), watch the exchange of money to pit one side against the other. It's always about the money and control.

The following is a compilation of data from the last good U. S. Census Bureau, U. S. Department of Health and Human Services (2016) and The Center for Immigration Studies (2016) that I've put into a simple chart.

2018 U.S. Census Bureau Data	Count	Percentage	# On Welfare	% of Race on Welfare	Welfare Expense
Population estimates, July 1, 2018, (V2018)	327,167,434				
Persons under 5 years	19,957,213	6.1%			
Persons under 18 years	73,285,505	22.4%			
Total Population > 18 years	233,924,715	71.5%			
Persons 65 years and over	52,346,789	16.0%			
Total U.S. spending on welfare annually:					$131,900,000,000
Americans > 18 Years On Welfare	110,489,000	35.4%			
Americans > 18 Years on Food Stamps	41,700,000	98.3%			
Americans > 18 Years on Unemployment Insurance	10,200,000	24.1%			
White Population	197,609,130	60.4%	42,869,732	21.7%	$51,177,200,000
Hispanic Population	52,673,957	16.1%	17,346,773	32.9%	$20,708,300,000
Black / African American	43,840,436	13.4%	43,974,622	100.3%	$52,496,200,000
Asian Population	19,302,879	5.9%	2,651,736	13.7%	$3,165,600,000
Native / Hawaiian and Other Populations	13,741,032	4.2%	3,646,137	26.5%	$4,352,700,000
Immigrants (est) - Legal and Illegal (not in U.S. Population)	42,400,000	13.0%	21,624,000	51.0%	Unknown

U. S. Population and Welfare Statistics (Compiled)

The Welfare numbers reflect the U. S. population of those 18 years and older. As you will notice, the Black/African American population on Welfare shows a greater than 100% ratio of the Census count, suggesting multiple accounts exist for many individuals since there are many successful African Americans in our nation not on Welfare. I'm sure the same goes for other categories but this is pretty telling. Obviously, many are gaming the system instead of adding value to others.

As Tocqueville noted, *"The American Republic will endure until the day Congress discovers that it can bribe the public with the public's money."* It would certainly seem that our U. S. Congress has mastered that tool!

Having no real program of integrating the newly released slaves after Emancipation and few having money, land or resources, these new citizens were destined to take the lowest paid and skilled labor jobs. Those hiring these new citizens certainly wanted to retain the status quo; a black slave populace.

In the late 1950's, President Dwight D. Eisenhower and the Republicans in Congress realized the evils that had continued throughout the South with segregation and political limitations imposed on the black community. In answer to this corruption, they put together the Civil

Rights Act of 1957 (the first since 1875), and though it was strongly opposed by nearly all southern Democrats in the House and Senate (including Lynden B. Johnson), the bill succeeded and was signed into law by President Eisenhower.

Though the law was enacted, few Southern Democrats at the federal level and within the southern State governments were willing to accept the new standard and fought against the inclusion of blacks into society and leadership. Southern Democrat leadership controlled all aspects of the community, and through their anger at the new law, reignited groups such as the Ku Klux Klan and other anti-negro factions.

During the 1960 election, Lynden Johnson was John Kennedy's primary contender for the Democratic Presidential ticket. Kennedy understood that to win the Texas and Southern Democrat vote, he would need Johnson on his team, so he offered Johnson to run as Vice President with him against Republican Richard M. Nixon. Johnson accepted, and the two narrowly won the Executive office.

It's said that Johnson was a tough and keen strategist, and with decades in politics, he was certainly one of the most powerful politicians in the United States. A devout southern Democrat, Johnson knew that Eisenhower's successful Civil Rights Bill and the Republican push for full integration, the newly empowered black Americans would vote Republican for years to come. **Johnson's answer was the most amazing strategy in our nation's history; to flip the black vote to the Democratic side, reversing the Emancipation Proclamation and Civil Rights Bill completely.**

Johnson understood Tocqueville's concept that *Congress* could *"bribe the public with the public's money."* He knew that he could use **handouts of public money** that would not only continue to segregate the black from white but could enslave the black community for a greater purpose than to just pick cotton – **Johnson could enslave them for their vote and decades of Democratic control!**

After the assassination of President Kennedy, Johnson took the helm and ushered in the *Great Society* and *War on Poverty*. These programs used tax-payer funds to push middle-class tax monies into urban and suburban minority districts while controlling the media through the (taxpayer funded) AP, NPR and PBS venues to promote his initiatives. The Johnson programs of Medicare, Medicaid and Aid to Education and Urban Development (AEUD) fit the narrative of flipping black voters almost instantly and completely to the Democratic Party. Hand-outs to the poor would ensure a poor slave populace for generations.

Instead of empowering these great citizens to pursue their Desire on the foundations of Hope, Opportunity, Purpose and Enthusiasm, Johnson instead offered a life of undeserved security that not only emasculated some of our greatest men but also reestablished the destructive practice of slave manipulation where the father is pulled from the home and encouraged to be irresponsible sexual predators. With Margaret Sanger's abortion on demand in the black community (Planned Parenthood), life had little meaning and threats of ever escaping were frowned on by everyone in the community. Becoming productive and honorable is touted as selling-out, caving into the white man's plan, and becoming an "Uncle Tom".

Johnson's *War on Poverty* has cost the U. S. taxpayer **$23 Trillion** since its adoption. Interestingly, our National Debt matches Johnson's war (enslavement plan) at **$23 Trillion** (as of this writing). As Johnson was quoted to have said, his *War on Poverty* would ensure a Democratic black vote for "the next 200 years", and true to his vision the black vote has hovered at 95% Democratic since enacting his *Welfare Program*.

My friend Clarence Mason Weaver is an amazing author and speaker on slavery in today's America. This *ex-Black Panther's* early books ***The Rope*** and ***It's OK to Leave the Plantation*** changed my perception on our nation's modern-day plantation and *slave master's* mentality. His book ***Tribalism*** should be mandatory reading in every Junior High and High School around the nation, and, in my opinion, would rock the world as a big screen movie! What an honorable example of a true American warrior!

Chapter 14 – Law and Order

Of all the dispositions and habits which lead to political prosperity, religion and morality are indispensable supports.... And let us with caution indulge the supposition that morality can be maintained without religion. George Washington

But it is religion and morality alone, which can establish the principles upon which freedom can surely stand. John Adams

Though good advice lies deep within the heart, a person with understanding will draw it out. Proverbs 20:5, NLT

~~~~~

Unfortunately, the Johnson Welfare programs have a much more detrimental intent than to just enslave our citizens. Going back to the Parable of the Talents shared earlier, there is honor and reward for those who use their talent for the betterment of the whole, while those who don't are cast into outer darkness. In the eyes of God and common sense, the servant who hides his talent is considered evil and wicked, and thereby judged harshly by the Master (Providence). I suggest that **without purpose there's perversion!**

Our Constitution and Cornerstones confirm that none in America should ever go hungry or lack the ability to pursue their desires and happiness if they don't reject our foundations. Sadly, evil *masters* have pervaded our societies creating unimaginable wealth for themselves by enslaving our most capable and talented, luring them in with a tantalizing momentary pleasure that enslaves for life. Such Master's suck the life from their slaves and then discard them as refuse when their value and usefulness is spent.

Pursuing a desire with honor is truly man's reason for life. When we pursue our dreams we not only attain blessings ourselves, we bless others, honor the Creator and add to the whole. When intended purpose and honor are rejected, it becomes every man for himself and taking from others is an easier path than earning it yourself. The *evil servant* in the story of the Talent throws all away because of a hate for the master who was willing to give him all he desired including honor. Yet he still hid his talent and survived by taking from others.

I put together the following chart using FBI data from 2016 for children under 18 years old. My apologies for the size, but I needed to show all the data so that it makes sense. **(DOWNLOAD A FREE E-VERSION TO SEE IT IN LARGER PRINT AND COLOR)**

The highlighted columns reflect the scale by race (per-capita) of the total offences defined on each line. In the colored version, RED highlights reflect the greater level of offences while GREEN reflects the lesser number of offences based on the per capita ration for each race. An example is that 60.4% of U. S. citizens are White/Caucasian, so the 419,393 offenses of the 788,064 by that race gives a "per capita" ratio of 0.9 (1.0 is mean).

2016 FBI Violent Criminal By Race = Under 18

Per Capita Ratio is Key with 1.0 being average ratio of offences. >1.0 = more offences per capita by race and <1.0 = less offences per capita	Total Offenses for All Races	White / Caucasian	Per Capita Ratio	Black / African	Per Capita Ratio	Latino / Hispanic	Per Capita Ratio	Asian	Per Capita Ratio	Indian / Alaskan	Per Capita Ratio	Hawaiian / Pac Isle	Per Capita Ratio
U.S. of U.S Populace by Race –	100%	60.4%		13.4%		16.1%		5.9%		2.7%		1.5%	
Total # of Offenses →	788,064	419,393	0.9	234,092	2.2	113,244	0.9	7,424	0.2	11,509	0.5	2,402	0.2
Murder / Manslaughter	782	244	0.5	413	3.9	103	0.8	11	0.2	9	0.4	2	0.2
Rape	3,355	1,877	0.9	956	2.1	455	0.8	31	0.2	23	0.3	13	0.3
Robbery	17,755	4,468	0.4	10,520	4.4	2,462	0.9	139	0.1	94	0.2	72	0.3
Aggravated assault	26,817	12,086	0.7	9,486	2.6	4,600	1.1	223	0.1	350	0.5	72	0.2
Burglary	30,234	14,036	0.8	10,606	2.6	4,874	1.0	302	0.2	351	0.4	65	0.1
Larceny-theft	121,169	63,842	0.9	38,364	2.4	15,155	0.8	1,672	0.1	1,754	0.5	382	0.2
Motor vehicle theft	14,517	5,810	0.7	6,255	3.2	2,123	0.9	106	0.1	190	0.5	33	0.1
Arson	2,281	1,409	1.0	486	1.6	298	0.8	31	0.2	48	0.8	9	0.3
Violent crime4	48,709	18,675	0.6	21,375	3.3	7,620	1.0	404	0.1	476	0.4	159	0.2
Property crime4	168,201	85,097	0.8	55,711	2.5	22,450	0.8	2,111	0.2	2,343	0.5	489	0.2
Other assaults	118,996	58,674	0.8	40,635	2.5	17,144	0.9	782	0.1	1,425	0.4	336	0.2
Forgery and counterfeiting	1,087	534	0.8	405	2.8	126	0.7	14	0.2	6	0.2	2	0.1
Fraud	4,030	1,818	0.7	1,745	3.2	384	0.6	29	0.1	49	0.5	5	0.1
Embezzlement	681	316	0.8	202	2.2	144	1.3	12	0.3	7	0.4	0	0.0
Stolen property	9,842	3,390	0.6	5,035	3.8	1,228	0.8	81	0.1	87	0.3	21	0.1
Vandalism	36,038	21,355	1.0	8,536	1.8	5,175	0.9	260	0.1	620	0.6	92	0.2
Illegal Weapons Posession	18,986	8,249	0.7	6,698	2.6	3,644	1.2	211	0.2	162	0.3	22	0.1
Prostitution / Commercialized vice	447	157	0.6	227	3.8	52	0.7	5	0.2	2	0.2	4	0.6
Sex offenses (not rape/prostitution)	7,937	4,786	1.0	1,707	1.6	1,278	1.0	85	0.2	62	0.3	19	0.2
Drug abuse violations	93,885	58,017	1.0	17,107	1.4	16,358	1.1	917	0.2	1,242	0.5	244	0.2
Gambling	224	50	0.4	150	5.0	21	0.6	3	0.2	0	0.0	0	0.0
Offenses against the family/children	3,009	1,596	0.9	646	1.6	306	0.6	17	0.1	443	5.5	1	0.0
Driving under the influence	6,036	4,499	1.2	338	0.4	977	1.0	73	0.2	132	0.8	17	0.2
Liquor laws	32,138	25,203	1.3	1,923	0.4	3,540	0.7	352	0.2	1,055	1.2	65	0.1
Drunkenness	5,158	3,132	1.0	373	0.5	1,405	1.7	46	0.2	194	1.4	8	0.1
Disorderly conduct	57,968	27,777	0.8	22,915	3.0	6,040	0.6	332	0.1	829	0.5	75	0.1
Vagrancy	710	368	0.9	220	2.3	102	0.9	7	0.2	11	0.6	2	0.2
All other offenses (except traffic)	142,016	80,504	0.9	37,132	2.0	20,306	0.9	1,375	0.2	1,938	0.5	761	0.4
Suspicion	82	34	0.7	33	3.0	8	0.6	4	0.8	0	0.0	3	2.4
Curfew and loitering law violations	31,884	15,162	0.8	10,979	2.6	4,936	1.0	304	0.2	426	0.5	77	0.2

Indian/Alaskan and Hawaiian/Pacific Island Population % from 2010 Census Data
Ethnicity totals represent those agencies that provided ethnicity breakdowns. Not all agencies provide ethnicity data.
Rape figures are aggregate totals of the data submitted based on both the legacy and revised UCR definitions.
Violent crimes are murder, nonnegligent manslaughter, rape, robbery, and aggravated assault. and arson.
Property crimes are offenses of burglary, larceny-theft, motor vehicle theft.

2016 FBI Data for Children < 18 years (Ratio Reflects Per Capita Offenses)

Note that the Asian and Hawaiian/Pacific Islanders show consistently low criminal activity. It's not biased data and has nothing to do with color but is a reflection on culture and environment. Our Asian cousins generally promote education and our Hawaiian/Pacific Island cousins enjoy their paradise, surf and sport. Freedom and hope create opportunity, while oppression normally opens the door for depravity.

Here are some specific concepts for our nation's children:

- White children with money have DUI challenges.
- White & Native American children have issues with alcohol/liquor.
- Native American children are a significant risk for abuse.
- Black/African children are 2 to 4 times as likely to commit a serious crime than White or Hispanic cousins, and up to 20 times as likely compared to the other cousins within the United States.

With freedom and purpose there's hope and opportunity, but without it there's contempt and corruption. Sadly, the statistics for those over 18 are similar (shown in Appendix II) meaning that we must provide a culture of freedom and hope for the children in order to change the culture of a people. President Johnson's plan to enslave the African American populace has certainly created a loyal voter block but has also established a detrimental reality for this powerful and passionate family of cousins. If Americans continue to allow this, promoting Black History Month while enslaving and dividing, our nation has no hope for her future, and the war Civil War will continue.

Thankfully, we have millions of champions like Clarence Weaver, Secretary Dr. Ben Carson, Herman Cain, Justice Clarence Thomas, Ambassador Alan Keyes and the beautiful and wise Candice Owens Farmer to prove it's not a color or race issue but a hope and pursuit issue.

Community	White / Caucasian	Hispanic / Latino	Black / African	Asian / Oriental	Native / Hawaiian	Total
Nationwide	197,609,130	52,673,957	43,840,436	19,302,879	13,741,032	327,167,434
Nationwide %	60.4%	16.1%	13.4%	5.9%	4.2%	100.0%
Institute for Diversity and Ethics in Sports	Golf = All American Golfers					
Football (NFL)	31.3%	0.8%	65.8%	1.3%	0.8%	100.0%
Baseball (MLB)	60.8%	27.9%	9.2%	1.3%	0.8%	100.0%
Basketball (NBA)	17.9%	2.9%	77.9%	0.8%	0.4%	100.0%
Soccer (MLS)	49.2%	25.0%	25.0%	0.8%	0.0%	100.0%
Golf (All)	79.0%	12.1%	5.1%	3.9%	0.0%	100.0%
Department of Labor & Statistics, U.S. Census						
Unemployment Rate (2017)	3.8%	5.1%	7.5%	3.2%	7.0%	
Education Levels (>100% = misunderstood question)						
No NH Diploma	15.6%	55.6%	15.6%	13.3%	Mixed w/ Others	
High School Diploma	24.8%	29.5%	29.5%	16.2%	Mixed w/ Others	
Some College	26.2%	24.6%	34.4%	14.8%	Mixed w/ Others	
Associates Degree	28.2%	23.1%	30.8%	17.9%	Mixed w/ Others	
Bachelors or Higher	26.5%	13.2%	19.9%	40.4%	Mixed w/ Others	
Total (Reflects Question Misunderstandng)	121.2%	146.0%	130.1%	102.6%	Mixed w/ Others	

Simple Pursuit Chart by Ethnicity (Wilson)
(*U. S. Census Bureau - Department of Labor & Statistics - ID&ES*)

Obviously, I love simple data charts where data sources validate one another. In the above chart, the Education question seeking the highest level of education shows 98% of Asians understood the question while Hispanics (English as a 2nd language) show a 46% misunderstanding. Other than that, I'm sure the other aspects of the chart are what we'd all expect considering the "communities" presented. With 5.9% of the U. S. population being Asian, these cousins represent the greatest percentages of the highly educated and thereby the greatest % of millionaires.

Due to President Johnson's strategy, our Black/African cousins living on the urban plantation resort to physical toughness as the perceived means of escape and proof of their power and purpose. Hence these warrior cousins (descended from Nimrod) naturally become exceptional athletes through inner-city athletic programs such as boxing, basketball and football. No prejudice or bias but a simple observation on the need for all humans to fulfill a purpose and to leverage their Ability, Skill and Opportunity (Talent).

Another aspect revealed in charts above and below is Johnson's Immigration and Nationality Act (INA) of 1965 which imported millions of needy, low wage welfare recipients from our southern nations. Like the Urban Plantations, these generally Hispanic cousins would mass together into Barrios around our nation taking low paying plantation (farming) jobs and leveraging our national welfare programs. Though unauthorized to vote, these new slaves illegally enroll on the Democratic roster by the millions.

"In 2012, 51% of households headed by an immigrant (legal or illegal) reported that they used at least one welfare program during the year compared to 30 percent of native households. Welfare in this study includes Medicaid and cash, food, and housing programs. Households headed by immigrants from Central America and Mexico (73 percent), the Caribbean (51 percent), and Africa (48 percent) have the highest overall welfare use." - U. S. Immigration Services

National expenses for these groups are obviously uncertain since most use an Individual Taxpayer Identification Number (ITIN) and do not pay into our Social Security or other tax systems while being allowed to submit tax claims for "Child Tax Credit" to the tune of $thousands per household whether the children exist or not. Their submitting for refunds at all is obviously illegal, and yet our overwhelmed Internal Revenue Service (IRS) is unable to adequately curtail the situation.

According to an October 2015 article by NPR, *59 million immigrants have moved to the United States making it the No. 1 immigrant destination on the planet since Johnson's INA.* Per Ice. Gov, *In Fiscal Year (FY) 2019, ICE's Enforcement and Removal Operations (ERO) officers arrested approximately 143,000 aliens and removed more than 267,000 – which is an increase in removals from the prior year. While the numbers of individuals apprehended or found inadmissible at the border nationwide increased 68% over the previous fiscal year, the total number of aliens arrested by ICE dropped by nearly 10% compared to FY 2018.* **More than 86% of those arrested by ICE had criminal convictions or pending charges.**

The Federation for American Immigration Reform (FAIR) Organization lists hundreds of deadly and scary crimes and attacks by illegal immigrants. With Sanctuary Cities protecting the illegal and blocking Federal agents from monitoring and managing, we are certainly seeing an uptick in danger from those within the Barrio Plantations around the nation.

Mind you, I am certainly not against immigration, and I'm confident that few American's are. Most of us can trace our roots back to a family member coming to America seeking freedom and opportunity, yet those who come into our nation or stay within our nation illegally are illegal. Those who promote open borders desire little more than to use such illegal individuals as a new component of slave and voting number while leveraging *false compassion* as a means of control. More on this topic in a later chapter.

Chapter 15 – Opportunities

There is no power on earth that can neutralize the influence of a high, simple and useful life. Booker T. Washington

The mystery of human existence lies not in just staying alive, but in finding something to live for. Fyodor Dostoyevsky

Let us not become weary in doing good, for at the proper time we will reap a harvest if we do not give up. Ga l 6:9, NIV

But as it is written, Eye hath not seen, nor ear heard, neither have entered into the heart of man, the things which God hath prepared for them that love him. 1 Cor 2:9, KJV

~~~~~~

Voyagers 1 and 2 recently passed beyond our Solar System (the Sun's Heliosphere) after being launched into space back in 1977. Amazingly, at 16 light hours from the Sun, we're still in touch with these extensions of mankind. More amazing is the concept that these spacecrafts of ours are only 1/50,000,000,000,000th of their way through our perceived 93 billion light-year-wide Universe, or like the width of a quarter on a trip from Earth to the Sun.

Of course, the term Universe can't be fully expressed in light years since the Greek term *Cosmos* implies *"the universe as a complex and orderly system or entity; the opposite of chaos"* (Wikipedia). On an even grander scale, many theorize of *multiverses* or other existences/times beyond our known dimensions and understanding. As we struggle with keeping our roads paved, how can any human even remotely suggest of our having ultimate intelligence? Our attempt with the Voyager crafts and the like are a perfect example of our limited understanding as we search out the concepts of existence. That said, I firmly believe we're meant to *seek* and *pursue* such mysteries!

Considering that mankind hasn't even scratched the surface of understanding existence or the opportunities within, why do we focus so much on limitations and lack of resources? I'll delve into the concepts of a global catastrophe, climate change and end-times in a later chapter, but for now I'd like to suggest that the *talents* given to mankind are all we need to preserve and protect life as we know it. Such talents of mankind make available resources unlimited.

Fear of diminishing resources is a means to control the masses!

We are all born with selfish desires and ambitions that must be conquered in order to become a *good and faithful servant*. Such challenges within our own nature require us to *champion ourselves* first, which helps us to become a champion for our family, community and humanity. Those who don't overcome their selfish nature eventually become worthless (a wicked servant) with limited value except as tools in the hands of the enemy.

He who has the gold makes the rules – he who makes the rules can take the gold – he who controls others can control both the gold and the rules.

We each have unique personalities, abilities, skills and talents that enable us to fit within humanity like a perfect puzzle piece. When others are permitted to control our shape (purpose), we lose the ability to fit within the puzzle, becoming bitter and vulnerable. From an early age something within us begs for purpose and value which if neglected or abused can harden the most precious of hearts. Hurting people hurt other people though any can change and become a hero for the hurting.

Pursuing our purpose (treasure) wears our rough edges down enabling us to fit perfectly in our place within life's puzzle. Being unique ensures a place of purpose like the ear and nose that have similar tissues but completely different functions. We each have a purpose that fulfills the body of mankind allowing us to search the depths of the soul and reach to the stars. If we accept who we are and encourage others to accept their pursuit of purpose (desires), we'd most certainly become a world of honor, hope and advancement. The reality remains that some care only for their own desires at the cost of others.

Let's use an example of this within the physiological realm. It's said that 99% of our body composition is oxygen, carbon, hydrogen, nitrogen, calcium, and phosphorus and that 0.85% is a combination of potassium, sulfur, sodium, chlorine, and magnesium. All of these exist naturally within our body and the universe (Cosmos) without chaos.

Though I believe that man was designed to think and create, I also believe that man's ability to manipulate creation often results in chaos and destruction. Scripture reveals the earliest humans lived nearly a thousand years without apparent disease or illness.

That said, it's evident that actions create reactions and certain chemical reactions begin within our Mother's womb through chemical reactions of balanced or imbalanced vitamins, minerals and heavy metals (copper, iron, zin, etc.). Though our bodies are made from all of these, having too much or too little throughout our lives creates imbalance. Since the earliest of times, men have been using metallurgy to create weapons, dishware and all sorts of things. Just like lead in paint was determined to cause illness in children, everything has the same potential for harm.

Cancer, for example, is the simple chemical reaction (corrosion) of foreign metals, minerals or other non-compliant element forced into the body through ingestion, application, inhalation or gestation. Improper innovations such as pewter, pesticides, genetically modified organism (GMO), cigarettes, excessive vitamins and a gazillion other unnatural products that man has created are surely the cause of all cancers and most diseases.

My bride constantly chastises me for drinking Diet Coke ® because it contains aspartame and acesulfame-k plus other unnatural chemicals. Although approved by the FDA it doesn't mean it's good, and I'm certain there's a detrimental chemical reaction to such chemicals (Alzheimer's, cancer, etc.) that are occurring in my body. But like smokers and drug addicts, we often do what we shouldn't.

Here's another glaring example - **anti-perspirants**. Along with disrupting the natural process of perspiration, these products present incompatible minerals/metals that are absorbed into the armpit and then accumulated within our bodies filters (glands) and nearby fatty tissue (the breasts). In time, these chemicals cause an undesired reaction (cancer) within the cells of these tissues. Though globally denied by healthcare professionals, I believe that breast cancer is the result of such an imbalance. This is where opportunity and pursuit must include responsibility and integrity.

Therefore, the greatest cancer in my opinion is the cancer of greed that continues to promote $gazillions in sales, treatment, and pretense of finding cures for cancer instead of discontinuing the product and finding a healthy alternative. Like so many global programs of selfish ambition - follow the money! We all know that manufacturers create and market harmful products just to keep the dollars flowing, while politicians and government agencies protect those who donate to their cause, knowing the harm. Our planet needs people of integrity who honor the Creator and His creation above the almighty dollar!

Another deadly "cancer" within society are the producers of pornography, sexual deviance and destructive movies, games and media. These people must be held accountable (financially and with jail time) for the crimes/evils perpetrated upon others for profit. While millions of our citizens champion the elimination of our Second Amendment right to bear arms, these same individuals not only permit but promote games, movies and shows that advance crimes and evils using guns and other weapons. Crime shows and movies have become more explicit and graphic in their presentation, glorifying evil and teaching new methods of perpetrating evil against others. Those who lack purpose and often the ones watching these programs instead of pursuing their purpose, creating a detrimental and deadly society.

Truth be told, the treasure map hidden within the cluttered artifacts of our mind must be searched-out, dusted off and pursued. Necessity, loss or desperation is often the force that causes us to seek the hidden folds of our lives in search of a greater purpose and destiny. It's during times of challenge that our senses are most receptive to our treasure's calling.

Financial gain (ROI) is certainly the benefit of creating a better mousetrap, and yet many mousetraps have been wholly designed to capture man himself. If *We the People* don't take ownership and responsibility for our nation's future, we will be forced to accept the consequences of our neglect. ***You can't expect what you don't inspect.***

Pursuing money isn't the key, pursuing purpose is. *"The little that a righteous man has Is better than the riches of many wicked. For the arms of the wicked shall be broken, But the Lord upholds the righteous."* (Psalms 37:16-17, NKJV).

Happiness can't be measured in wealth but in a worthy pursuit. Having a good heading *(Honor)*, seeking open doors *(Opportunity)*, understanding the value you offer *(Purpose)*, and maintaining a right attitude *(Enthusiasm)* will see you through will result in happiness. Though things seldom work out as planned, the pursuit and challenges encountered along the way make life exciting and takes us beyond our own vision. Following ***Desire and H.O.P.E.*** in honor of others will result in our achieving a higher level in life! Do this and we all win!

Chapter 16 –America's Citizenry

Injustice anywhere is a threat to justice everywhere. Martin Luther King, Jr.

Against the insidious wiles of foreign influence, (I conjure you to believe me fellow citizens) the jealousy of a free people ought to be constantly awake; since history and experience prove that foreign influence is one of the most baneful foes of Republican Government. George Washington

Let every person be subject to the governing authorities. For there is no authority except from God, and those that exist have been instituted by God. Rom 13:1, ESV

~~~~~

The strength and honor of the United States has been her avoidance of conquering and colonizing other nations while opening her doors to those who seek hope and opportunity. With a strong foundation built on our Cornerstones and Constitution, both her native children (Alaskan, Continental, and Hawaiian) and those seeking her freedoms from other nations (the rest of us) have been encouraged to retain and share the unique and colorful tapestry of cultures, traditions, spirit and foods. Examples are readily seen throughout our land in places such as Dutch/German farming areas, the various Chinatowns, Italian neighborhoods, and the great restaurants everywhere with Japanese, Indian, Mexican, German, Thai and so many other cuisines and cultures.

Regretfully, we've had an invasion of cultures intent on challenging and replacing our Cornerstones and Constitution with statutes such as **Communism** and **Sharia Law**. It is my opinion that these attempts are a form of treason or coup d'état that must be forcibly countered and done so quickly before they become viral. It's not that Islam or atheism are forbidden by any means, but their foundational laws and some practices are contrary to those established in the design of our nation.

Overall, this nation has been the most welcoming on Earth. She has continually opened her doors to millions of the world's *tired, poor and huddled masses*. Yet to our detriment, like the *Trojan Horse* of old, *Lady Liberty* has been used as a ploy in which millions of her nation's enemies have flooded through her gates seeking to suffocate this *one nation under God* rather than *yearning to breathe free*.

As mentioned previously, President Johnson and his Democrat majority (Senate and House) not only established our enslaving and detrimental Welfare System but also shredded our nation's security through their Immigration and Nationality Act (INA) of 1965. This Act effectively removed the protections of our long-standing American Immigration Law of 1924. The INA literally opened the floodgates to over 40 million immigrants, most who would fall captive to the Johnson Welfare plantation plan. These *imported immigrants* would become a new *counterculture* living in *barrios* or *slum plantations* throughout the land, where the only prerequisite is to vote for the Welfare/Slave party.

The following chart reveals the success of Johnson's plan:

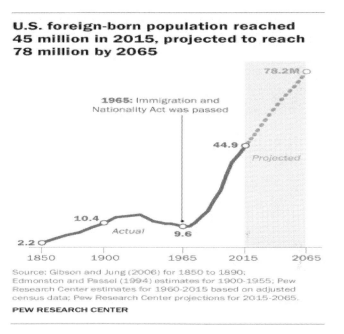

U.S. foreign-born population reached 45 million in 2015, projected to reach 78 million by 2065

1965: Immigration and Nationality Act was passed

78.2M

44.9

Projected

10.4

Actual

9.6

2.2

1850   1900   1965   2015   2065

Source: Gibson and Jung (2006) for 1850 to 1890; Edmonston and Passel (1994) estimates for 1900-1955; Pew Research Center estimates for 1960-2015 based on adjusted census data; Pew Research Center projections for 2015-2065.

PEW RESEARCH CENTER

Immigration Stats & Projections – Gibson and Jung

With the influx of immigrants through our southern border we have weakened our immigration policies and controls, enabling an invasion of violent criminals, drug cartels, child traffickers and murderous gangs. According to a 2010 United Nations report about 97% of the illegal immigrants who enter the U. S. clandestinely do so across the 2,000-mile border between the U. S. and Mexico. Though Democrats in Congress had no issues with Obama sending $billions to our nation's enemy Iran, they have continually denied President Trump's much smaller request to build a wall to secure our southern border

According to a Department of Homeland Security (DHS) 2012 study during the Obama Administration, greater than 46% of criminals deported in 2011 were previously deported and had illegally returned to the United States, which is a felony under federal law (Title 8 U. S. C. 1326). The Center for Immigration Studies (CIS) has suggested, *"The high percentage of repeat deportees is due in part to the ease of reentry to the United States for earlier deportees and the knowledge that if apprehended there is only a small chance that they will serve any prison time for that illegal reentry."* A 2013 Washington Times analysis of Immigration and Customs Enforcement (ICE) deportation numbers showed that deported Illegal Aliens with **criminal records** increased from 53% in 2012 to 55% in 2013.

A Government Accountability Office (GAO) study of 55,322 illegal aliens had an average of nearly eight arrests per illegal alien: 70% had between 2 and 10 arrests, with 26% (about 15,000) having 11 or more arrests. Drug and immigration offenses accounted for 45% of all offenses, and approximately 12% (over 6,600 illegal aliens) were arrested for violent offenses such as murder, robbery, assault, and sex-related crimes.

FBI crime studies also reveal heavy illegal alien involvement in national criminal activity:

- *75% of those on the most wanted criminals list in Los Angeles, Phoenix and Albuquerque are illegal aliens.*

- *25% of all inmates in California detention centers are Mexican nationals, as are more than 40% of all inmates in Arizona and 48% in New Mexico jails.*

- *Over 53% of all investigated burglaries reported in California, New Mexico, Nevada, Arizona, and Texas are perpetrated by illegal aliens.*

- *In Arizona 63% of cited drivers have no license, insurance or vehicle registration, with 97% being illegal aliens. New Mexico has a similar state with 66% of cited drivers in New Mexico have no license, insurance or vehicle registration, with 98% of those being illegal aliens.*

- *In January of 2015, California allowed illegal residents the ability to attain a driver's license, citing "By law, no one may discriminate against a holder of an AB-60 license, or use this license to attempt to question the holder's citizenship or immigration status."*

U. S. Border Patrol statistics thankfully show a decline in Illegal Alien activity within the United States under the *Wild Card* Administration:

	FY16	FY17	FY18	FY 19	FY20 TD DEC
U.S. Border Patrol Criminal Alien Arrests	12,842	8,531	6,698	4,269	787

	FY16	FY17	FY18	FY19	FY20 TD DEC
Assault, battery, domestic violence	1,007	692	524	299	37
Burglary, robbery, larceny, theft, fraud	825	595	347	184	40
Driving under the influence	2,458	1,596	1,113	614	118
Homicide, manslaughter	8	3	3	2	0
Illegal drug possession, trafficking	1,797	1,249	871	449	96
Illegal entry, re-entry	7,060	4,502	3,920	2,663	466
Illegal weapons possession, transport, trafficking	237	173	106	66	10
Sexual offenses	155	137	80	58	13
Other 1	2,544	1,851	1,364	814	158

Fiscal Year 2020 runs October 01, 2019 - September 30, 2020.
[1] "Other" includes any conviction not included in the categories above.

U.S. Border Patrol enforcement actions related to arrests of criminal aliens for Fiscal Years 2016 - 2019 and FY 2020 (YTD)

As noted earlier, *"In 2012, 51% of households headed by an immigrant (legal or illegal) reported that they used at least one welfare program during the year compared to 30% of native households."*

With immigration strategies since the Johnson era, thousands of support organizations have been established to help legal and illegal aliens "game the system". Not all are corrupt or anti-American, but I can guarantee that the end-goal of nearly all is to promote a Democratic party vote. I personally receive monthly updates from the Pennsylvania Immigration and Citizenship Coalition (PICC) who literally set tables up at *Citizenship Swearing-in ceremonies*, immediately registering them to vote (Democrat of course) and receive information to attain as much government assistance as possible. They are then encouraged to share the information to legal and illegal friends. And this isn't hearsay, I've personally witnessed these efforts in Philadelphia, PA.

A 2017 study by the Center for Immigration Studies (CIS) suggests that the fiscal cost created by illegal immigrants as being $746.3 billion compared to a total cost of deportation of $124.1 billion. The National Academies of Sciences, Engineering, and Medicine (NASEM) has estimated the lifetime fiscal impact (taxes paid minus services used) of immigrants, and using those estimates has determined a net fiscal drain of $65,292 per illegal — excluding costs for their children.

Obama's U. S. Secretary of Homeland Security Janet Napolitano used her prosecutorial discretion to create the *Deferred Action for Childhood Arrivals* (DACA) program to defer proceedings against *"DREAMers"* (children born in the U. S. to legal and illegal parents) which allows them to stay in the United States without fear of deportation. Amazingly, Napolitano then identified our Armed Forces Veterans as a *"Homeland Security Threat"* due to their potential *"Rightwing Extremism"*. Such perverted standards by a U. S. Secretary confirms the seriousness of the threat against our national values and the need for immediate redress of our immigration policies.

Here's a more concerning immigration act perpetrated *against* our nation by the Obama Administration – The *Import and Sanctuary Placement* of millions of individuals from anti-American nations. Mind you, most of the imported individuals have been intentionally hidden, untracked and strategically placed within our nation. Though some are known, most are an unknown as far as who they are, where they came from and where they are at today. Though uncertain of the number, it's believed to exceed 1,000,000 people.

As an example, the CIS estimates that more than 100,000 Somalian refugees were imported and placed in strategic "districts" around our nation. Though 10% of the population in Somalia is Christian (and the most persecuted of her people), the Obama Administration intentionally imported 99% that hold to the Muslim faith. Is it any wonder that our *Sanctuary Cities* saw the 2018/2019 elections of numerous Muslims to our highest offices - 4 to the House of Representatives, 3 to the State Senate and 10 to the respective State House? Obviously, this was an intentional act like the establishment of our slums and barrios yet with a more dangerous intent and result.

Mind you, our Constitution and founding principles wholly support anyone of any religion to live and serve our nation, yet this was a strategic initiative with a strategic intent. James Clapper (previous Director of U. S. National Intelligence) said that ISIS is "taking advantage of the torrent of migrants to insert operatives into that flow."

Though many of our recent immigrants actively pursue the demise of our nation's Cornerstones and Constitution, most Americans are grateful for the opportunities offered by Lady Liberty. Truly, her doors are open to the tired, poor and huddled masses yearning to be free but not at the expense of her own demise.

We can't expect what we don't inspect!

Chapter 17 – America in the Universe

Give me your tired, your poor, your huddled masses yearning to breathe free, the wretched refuse of your teeming shore. Send these, the homeless, tempest-tossed to me, I lift my lamp beside the golden door! Emma Lazarus, Statue of Liberty

Some of you were prisoners suffering in deepest darkness and bound by chains, because you had rebelled against God Most High and refused his advice. You were worn out from working like slaves, and no one came to help. You were in serious trouble, but you prayed to the Lord, and he rescued you. He brought you out of the deepest darkness and broke your chains. Psalms 107:10-14, CEV

~~~~~

Just as America has been a Melting Pot for freedom seekers from around the globe, she has also been a catalyst for freedom and hope around the globe. As history reveals, no nation can boast of being perfect or truly good, yet it's my belief that America was established by God as a light in a darkened world. And though her light has dimmed and even flickered at times, I still believe this One Nation under God is being held aloft as a light on the hill for the world, at least for the time being. Her flame being kindled by prayer, integrity and goodness.

The 2006 movie *Amazing Grace* by Michael Apted is a beautiful and accurate depiction of the decades long campaign of William Wilberforce (Ioan Gruffudd) and Prime Minister William Pitt (Benedict Cumberbatch) to abolish the slave trade in the British Empire. Wilberforce's relationship with John Newton, the repentant slave trader and author of our beloved hymn *Amazing Grace*, literally ushered in the end of slavery throughout the western world. This humbling glimpse into the heart of man is a revelation of both his evil and compassionate nature. Although America is not a focus of the movie, there's a hint that our Declaration was a factor in the demise of the British Empire's slave-trade that would eventually return to our own shores through Lincoln.

Slavery had been a continual evil throughout the recorded history of man. The Torah given to Moses and America's Constitution have been the strongest laws given to man that address this atrocity. Still, it took men of honor such as Moses, Pitt, Wilberforce and Lincoln, committed to God and man, to battle for their brothers against the powerful. As Britain and Wilberforce leveraged the Cornerstones of America's republic, the Republican Party and Abraham Lincoln eventually leveraged England's honor to finally end our official position on slavery. Though Britain and America have been common examples of fallen mankind, these nations have also given rise to heroes around the globe who would champion the rights of others.

Inspired by Britain's Wilberforce and America's Lincoln, the French poet Édouard de Laboulaye encouraged the French sculptor Frédéric Bartholdi of Paris to work with the United States on creating our *Statue of Liberty* as a monument to renounce Napoleon's tyrannical European campaign and as a symbol of freedom for the world. Our *Lady* reflects the ancient Roman symbol *Libertas* who holds a torch over a path for those who seek liberty and hope while cradling a book representing our *Declaration of Independence* (July 4, 1776) and *Constitution*.

Though an imperfect nation of imperfect people, America's Cornerstones, Constitution and standards have been a foundation and blessing to millions within her own borders and to billions of others around the world. With ample occasions and power to expand her footprint around the globe, Lady Liberty has instead promoted independence and sovereignty for all, not in word alone but in action. Her sacrifices to ensure liberty for all have left the blood of her own children on the battlefields of foreign nations on almost every continent. America has avoided the path of colonization and instead allowed her light to shine freely for the world to see as an example of God's providence.

There are two distinct lenses through which we can view our nation and the world: the lens of hope, honor and opportunity, or the lens of disdain, revenge and control. The lens chosen by an individual, community or nation determines their actions and future. America and most of her people have commonly chosen to see things through the lens of hope, honor and opportunity, championing these causes within her own shores and around the globe. Though never perfect, she has routinely stood on the high ground of such characteristics.

Sadly, as our flame has been darkened by a veil brought to our own shores by our nation's enemies, we see that a darkness has increasingly shrouded the world with uncertainty. The recent challenges to our Nation's Cornerstones and Foundations by those with Marxism and Jihadist intentions, have caused concerns worldwide. Efforts to distort our histories, challenge our standards and weaken our resolve of hope and honor have certainly taken their toll. Those whose intent is to extinguish our light of liberty and to leverage our national strength for their personal gain have done so while standing on the very Cornerstones and foundation they hope to destroy.

As noted earlier, a recent example of a targeted attack against our foundations was the clandestine shipments of $billions to our nation's enemies (Iran and China) by the Obama Administration have enabled each to create greater weaponry for use against our own shores. Frightening is the fact that dozens of similar acts have occurred using *We the People's* money against her own people, attacking our freedoms and weakening our defenses. Thankfully, the *Trump Card* was cast on the table at the last minute, or America could well be playing her final hand.

As President Lincoln envisioned 150 years ago, Lady Liberty has quietly wrapped a noose around her own neck by prostituting herself to nations whose intent is to kill, steal and destroy her posterity. The foundations on which she has established her freedoms and glory have become the harlot's bed on which she's opened her skirt to those who would abuse her beauty and long-lost innocence.

Yet hope is not lost! Though we've acted as a prostitute and allowed complacency to blanket our land, we are also witnessing a nation that has fallen on her knees before a benevolent Creator asking in earnest prayer for the chance to rebuild our Cornerstones, reestablish our integrity and to once again shine our light to the world. Much like the hearts of the people during the time of Lincoln, we are at a point of balance that could readily destroy our nation or unite her in honor. The question is, on which side of our *Lady Liberty's* scales will we (her people) place our worth, our lives, and our sacred honor?

My hope and prayer are that the hearts of our national and global leaders in government, media, education, enterprise and finance, will be revealed for who they are. That a visible and vivid separation is revealed between those desiring power and those desiring hope and honor. As this separation is revealed, I also pray that those of honor would boldly stand against those with evil and tyrannical intent both within our nation and around the globe, and champion the causes of Life, Liberty and Pursuit of Happiness. **To rekindle our Lady's light!**

Conversely, **Socialism** is the *sales tactic* used by those desiring to control the masses. History proves that those selling the concept of a utopian world of shared resources are only deceiving the masses for their personal gain. As Tytler suggests, human nature seeks the easy and selfish path instead of the right one, electing instead to float downstream like a dead fish while the net of the elite waits at the most opportune point. As seen today, the division between our two primary political parties couldn't be any wider, with the Democrats touting Socialism and global takeover, and the Republicans touting Nationalism and Capitalistic progress.

In order for the Democratic plan of Socialism to succeed they must first control the finances (note the stock market manipulation) and then regulate the "river of freedom" by removing all threats to their power, such as the Second Amendment right to defend against a tyrannical government. It's then an easy task to control all buying, selling and property ownership and to establish a national police force (Gestapo type) with which to ensure full control by the chosen elite.

As noted by Tytler, a democratic body of any kind will eventually relinquish freedom to the inevitable bonds of slavery. An example is our relationship within the United Nations where the U. S. funds 22% of the U. N. budget and yet has the same single vote as struggling dictatorships and communist nations. As it is today, the collective vote of the U. N. is continually in opposition of our American Cornerstones, Constitution and intent, and seems solely focused on the control or diminishment of our nation and her allies. Like panhandlers on our street corners, nations beg for American handouts while hating her for her success. When America suggests that all can pursue prosperity, health and pursuit, many become angry and vindictive with some seeking our demise.

Had we elected to jump off the *Hilarious Cliff* in 2016, there is no doubt in my mind that *Clinton's* first pursuits (if accompanied by a Democrat House) would have been to remove our First and Second Amendment rights. It may have been a challenge, but with the powers of her *Deep State* and identifications from Facebook, Google and Twitter, they would have known the opposition and gone after it directly. After removing all opposition, it would have been a simple task to relinquish our American sovereignty to the United Nations. *We the People* would have floated down the stream from complacency into slavery within a few short years.

If *Clinton* had been elected in 2016, I'm convinced that she would have quickly nominated **Mr. Obama** as the first American *President of the United Nations General Assembly*. With Clinton relinquishing American sovereignty to the U. N., Obama would have become the most powerful ruler in the history of the world, having access to all of America's and combined U.N. national resources, technology and military. We're not out of the woods just yet, as the wicked queen still holds a poisoned apple prepared and shined-up for us to bite.

It's certainly evident that a *Deep State* exists and is much deeper than anything any of us could have imagined. The fake Clinton FBI Investigation permitting the destruction of emails, texts and hardware revealed the boldness of this *Deep State*. Even today, our media dismisses the DNC/Clinton funded *Steele Dossier* that lead to the illegal FISA Warrant with 17 proven violations. This illegal FISA then prompted the illegal *Crossfire Hurricane* FBI Investigation by Obama spying on and attacking Candidate/President *Trump* and his supporters from 2016 to 2019. Even with confirmation of these illegal tactics by both Special Council Mueller and FBI Inspector General Horowitz, the Democratic Congress pursued an Impeachment for Trump upon these illegal actions. Sadly, though they each exonerating the *Trump Card*, they also made sure to exonerate their own Deep State players coordinating the coup d'état such as the FBI leaders, Clinton, the DNC and mainstream Media.

It's hugely evident that a few or many are manipulating world dynamics in order to usher in the Obama/Clinton plan. With the unprecedented fear and panic of the so-called Corona Virus, which has nearly "zero effect" except to kill an already ill and/or elderly populace, something more serious is occurring. There appears to be those pulling the strings unconcerned about the harm caused to the American and world populace. Someone is seeking power and control, and the people are willingly swimming with the current towards the net that they have staged.

I am so very amazed that every news outlet on every possible media venue is talking about nothing but the Corona Virus, while as of this writing (mid-March 2020) and in the span of months, there are still less than **200,000 cases,** a recovery of nearly 100,000 and less than 1,000 deaths, with some 80+% being the elderly (over 70 years old), and nearly 99% having a deadly pre-existing condition. I'm not even confident about the WHO and CDC numbers as being valid! In my opinion, this virus is the next attack against Trump and his growing economy, destroying his success just before the **2020 elections**.

This is a similar event to what happened in the Roaring 1920's under Republican President Herbert Hoover. The market and hopes were high, America was building, and the global economy was abounding, then something that nobody can explain caused the Stock Market to drop and the people to panic. The Great Depression and WWII came upon the world with little concern or thought as to "why". The thing is that the Democrats (who again owned the media even back then) promoted a man named Roosevelt to rescue the nation and world.

Roosevelt and the Democratic Party won a huge victory, took over the United States, and established our strategic Welfare System. The Democrat Party remained in control for generations and weren't challenged until Eisenhower, Reagan and now Trump. The same scenario happened in a lighter fashion at the end of G. W. Bush's 2ⁿᵈ term when, for some reason, a modestly strong Market all of a sudden crashed as "someone" began to offload their shares, causing the *"Bush Recession"* and ushering in Barrack Hussain Obama as President.

Today, it seems as though the entire world is against our generation, and unfortunately, many are responding like the Germans and Russians did when they put their own comforts and security ahead of the comforts and security of their posterity. They simply cowered down and allowed the evil forces to take control of their freedoms and lives, forgetting the nobility of their past. We know how that turned-out, and I hope you'll join me in boldly confronting this similar tactic within our nation.

COVID-19, the global economy and near Martial Law are certainly challenging our very existence, but if we reject the panic, identify the manipulators, and regain our balance as a people of this *"one nation under God",* I believe we can survive. As alluded throughout this manuscript, America was established by the *God of nature, and nature's God* as a beacon to the world. If *we the people* redirect our compass back to our founding Cornerstones and pursue the *God of Nature's* standards, I've no doubt that we can once again rise as a City on the Hill, sharing our light of freedom to the entire world.

Chapter 18 – A Good Defense

War is an ugly thing, but not the ugliest of things: the decayed and degraded state of moral and patriotic feeling which thinks that nothing is worth a war, is much worse. John Stuart Mills

Call upon Me in the day of trouble; I shall rescue you, and you will honor Me. Psalms 50:15, NAS

Vindicate me, my God, and plead my cause against an unfaithful nation. Rescue me from those who are deceitful and wicked. Psalm 43:1, KJV

~~~~~

The United States is obviously not alone on this sea of humanity, with our National Defense extending beyond our borders and to nations around the globe. As populations and technologies grow the global neighborhood shrinks with external forces continuously challenging our defenses, political strength, finances and every aspect of our posture. These challenges come not just daily, but every minute and second. Our successes, resources and revenues are like money dangling from the pocket of a drunk sailor, free pickings for the shrewd and nearly indefensible.

"Bad men need nothing more to compass their ends, than that good men should look on and do nothing". Attributed to both Edmund Burke, and John Stuart Mills (specifically), this statement lays the evils within our borders at the feet of good Americans who do nothing. Mr. Burke also suggests that *"when a separation is made between liberty and justice, neither is safe".*

I'm certainly not a military strategist, though I do have many years of experience within our military and Department of Defense (DoD). It's my strong opinion that much like every government program, our military is replete with Fraud, Waste and Abuse (FWA), not completely by intent but by inheritance, false zeal and of course political gain.

Our military has many antiquated strategies and assets which need to be replaced, removed or enhanced in order to eliminate excess and unnecessary maintenance/management, both hard and soft assets such as programs, equipment and people. As proposed in the 2018 Summary of the National Defense Strategy (signed by then Secretary of Defense,

James Mattis), "Sharpening the American Military's Competitive Edge" should always be our target. We need to hone down our military and its footprint to a sharper and more effective asset. Here's my thoughts, coinciding and expanding on Secretary Mattis' proposed strategy:

- Modernize Nuclear capabilities and infrastructure,
- Expand Space Force strategies and capabilities,
- Expand Cyberspace/Communication domains and capabilities,
- Improve and modernize Missile defense,
- Refocus Joint Force capabilities while retaining specialty sectors to limit waste and redundancy,
- Increase Special Operations/Forces capabilities,
- Establish a greater Forward Posture, with streamlined reactive capabilities and stations within ally territories,
- Remove assets from non-ally territories (such as Afghanistan),
- Enhance and expand Advanced autonomous (AI) systems.
- Enhance agile Forward Logistics, Support & Medical profiles,
- Destroy or repurpose old and obsolete arms and assets,
- Reduce Active Military and increase Guard/Reserve personnel,
- Transfer stateside DoD, VA, PHS hospital services and health personnel to civilian sector healthcare systems,
- Activate a National Service Act (NSA) for 2-years of service with DoD, Public Safety, Infrastructure & Global outreach.

I believe the current Defense strategy is well defined and funded, albeit our overall defense posture is aged, obese and wasteful. Like all government managed programs, our footprint is too large and our reach too short. Emphasis should focus on reduced assets and expanded capabilities as well as Research and Development (R&D) with lighter and more responsive profiles. Serious measures must be taken to eliminate FWA and program redundancies between services while streamlining and enhancing proficiencies.

Every American at the age of 17/18 needs to serve America for 2-years in a Federal Branch of our government (Defense, Education, Health & Human Services, Homeland Security, etc.) or international service program such as the Peace Corps. Serving our nation and its citizenry away from home will expand understanding, increase opportunities and create a national comradery that benefits the nation as a whole. After 2 years of service (with commensurate pay), individuals would qualify for 2 years of college or technical school education and receive a limited stipend.

I firmly believe this program would be our nation's greatest opportunity for both her citizenry and future. Such an initiative would:

- Rebuild our national pride,
- Diminish prejudices and enhance comradery,
- Dissolve slave plantations in slums and barrios,
- Decrease/end our national drug epidemic,
- Reduce criminal activities throughout our nation,
- Enhance our nations defenses and infrastructure,
- Provide a skilled labor force for future generations,
- Help to reduce our national debt,
- Build a nation of honorable citizenry,

The *Trump Card* is being played to *"Keep America Great"* which empowers government and commercial entities to refocus on internal strengths. Though challenged by many who desire a more globally dependent platform for America, our nation's well-being is essential to the survival of the free world. A healthy foundation allows for healthy growth. A strong stance allows for greater reach, and the world needs the support and hand of friendship from this *one nation under God.*

Sadly, just as our nation's enemies have embedded themselves within our highest and most critical offices, these same enemies have cracked open the armor of our nation's military posture allowing evils within the ranks of our nation's defenders. As seen in 2009, U. S. Army Major Nidal Hasan murdered 13 of his fellow soldiers and injured more than 30 others in a mass shooting attack at Fort Hood. Classified as workplace violence, it should be terrorism and treason with Hasan being executed long ago, yet he remains in prison on our tax dollars. His supervisors and the Army knew of Hasan's disdain for America and his fellow soldiers, but did not intervene.

A similar attack recently occurred at NAS Pensacola, Florida by Saudi 2ndLt Mohammed Alshamrani, killing 3 service members and injured 8 others while attending a U. S. military flight training program. Events such as these should never occur. Military bases must establish armed control to prevent internal attacks.

With our military being politically and physically disarmed on our stateside bases, our last Administration further disarmed our nation's defenders at home and abroad by placing them in harm's way with dangerous *rules of engagement* restrictions. Simply put, America's military and law enforcement personnel have been pushed to the frontlines with their hands zip tied. While expecting them to sacrifice their own lives for ours, many in leadership have constrained and limited their defenses while scrutinizing and condemning their actions through the lens of political correctness (PC). The media is the greatest accuser of those who give their all for the freedoms of our citizenry as they propagate information that jeopardizes these heroes.

Again, many of our nation's enemies have embedded themselves within places of power throughout our government, intent on weakening our national strength and dismantling the physical and legal protections of our military, borders and law enforcement. Congressional leaders and others who've sworn to protect and defend our nation, have instead taken their efforts to attack those in the trenches. We as the *Board of Directors* must hold our *Congress* and other leaders to their oath and root out those who subvert our laws with an intent to destroy/diminish our nation. This includes all government offices, with the strongest judgements against those in high positions such as members of Congress, the State Department, Department of Justice, the FBI and similar entities. Double standards must be eradicated, and strong justice implemented.

As suggested, Fraud, Waste and Abuse (FWA) are rampant throughout our military and our government in general. The expenses and losses due to FWA could easily fund a rapid and judicious program of assessment throughout. Having served for over 40 years in uniform and civilian attire, I can tell you wholeheartedly that FWA not only exists at all levels, but that it thrives with Congress being one of our greatest perpetrators.

Examples of FWA are Naval Stations Pascagoula, MS and Mobile, AL, where a military build-up under President Reagan (Dem Congress) cost $billions in the mid 1980's, only to be closed by Clinton in the 2000's. Pascagoula was a 187 acre fully operational Naval Base with a state of art 3-mile long causeway, built on Singing Island. The entire base and causeway were "donated" to the state of Mississippi.

Without inspection, there's deception!

Throwing money at ineffective programs doesn't fix the problem. External assessments and audits by unbiased and yet knowledgeable individuals are a must for every government program. Tenure is a questionable qualification at best. Establishing the same retirement posture for all government employees like those pushed on the civilian sector will ensure a responsible and productive workforce. Outdated and unnecessary government services must be cut as soon as possible in order to fully support productive and efficient programs. Like technology, government programs should strive to be smaller and more effective.

Stateside Military, Veteran's Administration (VA) and Public Health Services (PHS) hospitals and clinics cost $billions every year in new construction, equipage and maintenance, often redundant by a nearby civilian healthcare facility. As seen in recent reports, government owned/operated Health Systems results in deficient, outdated and detrimental healthcare services. The DoD Tricare program is a successful example of partnering the military healthcare needs with the competent/state-of-art civilian healthcare sector. Transitioning all stateside government health services to civilian hospitals/clinics with partner oversight agreements will ensure optimal health services for all.

Limited and antiquated services within our DoD health programs have also hampered our front-line health professionals (doctors, nurses and medics) for optimum readiness. Being assigned to state-of-the-art civilian sector hospitals in emergency, operating, laboratory, radiology and other disciplines, will ensure a competent provider in the field. This is a great example where a diminished Active and expanded Reserve Military footprint would be justified. The fiscal savings from decreased construction, outfitting and management of stateside hospitals/clinics could then be redirected towards better training and equipage of our frontline assets.

Government healthcare is one example of the many outdated and wasteful programs that could easily and successfully be replaced. As we've seen by Elon Musk's Space Exploration Technologies Corp. (SpaceX), joint ventures between Private Capital entities and government programs are greatly successful and reduce FWA. Our national defense and offence depend on improved policies, actions and audits.

Chapter 19 – A Healthy Nation

Government is not a solution to our problem; government is the problem... Government does not solve problems; it subsidizes them. Government's view of the economy could be summed up in a few short phrases: If it moves, tax it. If it keeps moving, regulate it. If it stops moving, subsidize it. ... The problem is not that people are taxed too little; the problem is that government spends too much. Ronald Reagan

For where your treasure is, there your heart will be also". Matt 6:21, KJV

~~~~~

Is the United States a healthy nation? Obviously, the earlier chapters reveal my belief that she is not. Can we be healed? Absolutely, but it necessitates a repentant and courageous heart. America has sadly placed her treasure in many evil purposes.

OMB Federal Surplus/Deficit By Fiscal Year

				($ Millions) Surplus / Deficit					($ Millions) Surplus / Deficit
FY	President	Senate	House		FY	President	Senate	House	
1964	Johnson	Dem	Dem	5,915	1992	Bush Sr.	Dem	Dem	269,238
1965	Johnson	Dem	Dem	1,411	1993	Clinton	Dem	Dem	290,321
1966	Johnson	Dem	Dem	3,698	1994	Clinton	Dem	Dem	255,051
1967	Johnson	Dem	Dem	8,643	1995	Clinton	Rep	Rep	203,186
1968	Johnson	Dem	Dem	25,161	1996	Clinton	Rep	Rep	163,952
1969	Nixon	Dem	Dem	3,242	1997	Clinton	Rep	Rep	107,431
1970	Nixon	Dem	Dem	2,842	1998	Clinton	Rep	Rep	21,884
1971	Nixon	Dem	Dem	23,033	1999	Clinton	Rep	Rep	69,270
1972	Nixon	Dem	Dem	23,373	2000	Clinton	Rep	Rep	125,610
1973	Ford	Dem	Dem	14,908	2001	Bush Jr.	Rep	Rep	236,241
1974	Ford	Dem	Dem	6,135	2002	Bush Jr.	Rep	Rep	128,236
1975	Ford	Dem	Dem	53,242	2003	Bush Jr.	Rep	Rep	157,758
1976	Ford	Dem	Dem	73,732	2004	Bush Jr.	Rep	Rep	377,585
1977	Carter	Dem	Dem	14,744	2005	Bush Jr.	Rep	Rep	412,727
1978	Carter	Dem	Dem	54,659	2006	Bush Jr.	Rep	Rep	318,346
1979	Carter	Dem	Dem	59,185	2007	Bush Jr.	Rep	Dem	248,181
1980	Carter	Dem	Dem	40,726	2008	Bush Jr.	Rep	Dem	160,701
1981	Reagan	Rep	Dem	73,830	2009	Obama	Dem	Dem	458,553
1982	Reagan	Rep	Dem	78,968	2010	Obama	Dem	Dem	1,412,688
1983	Reagan	Rep	Dem	127,977	2011	Obama	Dem	Rep	1,294,373
1984	Reagan	Rep	Dem	207,802	2012	Obama	Dem	Rep	1,299,599
1985	Reagan	Dem	Dem	185,367	2013	Obama	Dem	Rep	1,076,573
1986	Reagan	Dem	Dem	212,308	2014	Obama	Dem	Rep	679,775
1987	Reagan	Dem	Dem	221,227	2015	Obama	Rep	Rep	484,793
1988	Reagan	Dem	Dem	149,730	2016	Obama	Rep	Rep	441,960
1989	Bush Sr.	Dem	Dem	155,178	2017	Trump	Rep	Rep	594,651
1990	Bush Sr.	Dem	Dem	152,639	2018	Trump	Rep	Dem	665,446
1991	Bush Sr.	Dem	Dem	221,036	2019	Trump	Rep	Dem	779,138

OMB Federal Surplus/Deficit (1964-2019) – (Wilson Format),

The above chart reveals a habitual overspending and irresponsible government over the last 60 years and has been the case since FDR and before. Overall, it's hard to identify a variance based on political party because the party obviously doesn't matter. Both spend what they don't have revealing a careless attitude about future generations.

That said, there is a glaring anomaly shown during *Fiscal Years (FYs) 1998-2002* reflecting a significant flip from the common *deficit* of around **$300B** to a *surplus* of nearly **$300B**.

The unique difference during this Republican lead Congress and Clinton (Democrat) Presidency was Newt Gingrich's *"Contract with America"*. Although there was a Party split between the President and Congress, it's my firm belief that the Impeachment indictment of then President Bill Clinton forced him to accept the *Contract with America* as submitted, upholding *Accountability, Responsibility and Opportunity* for our nation. Here's a simple summary of the proposed Contract as presented during a September 27, 1994 press conference:

1. The Fiscal Responsibility Act

A balanced budget/tax limitation amendment and a legislative line-item veto to restore fiscal responsibility to an out-of-control Congress, requiring them to live under the same budget constraints as families and businesses.

2. The Taking Back Our Streets Act

An anti-crime package including stronger truth-in-sentencing, "good faith" exclusionary rule exemptions, effective death penalty provisions, and cuts in social spending from this summer's "crime" bill to fund prison construction and additional law enforcement to keep people secure in their neighborhoods and kids safe in their schools.

3. The Personal Responsibility Act

Discourage illegitimacy and teen pregnancy by prohibiting welfare to minor mothers and denying increased AFDC for additional children while on welfare, cut spending for welfare programs, and enact a tough two-years-and-out provision with work requirements to promote individual responsibility.

4. The Family Reinforcement Act

Child support enforcement, tax incentives for adoption, strengthening rights of parents in their children's education, stronger child pornography laws, and an elderly dependent care tax credit to reinforce the central role of families in American society.

5. The American Dream Restoration Act

A $500 per child tax credit, begin repeal of the marriage tax penalty, and creation of American Dream Savings Accounts to provide middle class tax relief.

6. The National Security Restoration Act

No U. S. troops under U. N. command and restoration of the essential parts of our national security funding to strengthen our national defense and maintain our credibility around the world.

7. The Senior Citizens' Fairness Act

Raise the Social Security earnings limit which currently forces seniors out of the work force, repeal the 1993 tax hikes on Social Security benefits and provide tax incentives for private long-term care insurance to let Older Americans keep more of what they have earned over the years.

8. The Job Creation and Wage Enhancement Act

Small business incentives, capital gains cut and indexation, neutral cost recovery, risk assessment/cost-benefit analysis, strengthening the Regulatory Flexibility Act and unfunded mandate reform to create jobs and raise worker wages.

9. The Common-Sense Legal Reform Act

"Loser pays" laws, reasonable limits on punitive damages and reform of product liability laws to stem the endless tide of litigation.

10. The Citizen Legislature Act

A first-ever vote on term limits to replace career politicians with citizen legislators. Instruct the House Budget Committee to report to the floor and we will work to enact additional budget savings, beyond the budget cuts specifically included in the legislation described above, to ensure that the Federal budget deficit will be less than it would have been without the enactment of these bills.

As Speaker of the House, Newt Gingrich said in a public-television interview, God had given him a mission: *"To find honest self-government and to survive as a free people."* As such, Congress attained a near or better than 2/3 approval on all initiatives in both houses. Those initially vetoed by President Clinton were lightly adjusted and then later signed into law.

We the People must once again accept responsibility to hold our *Elected Officials* accountable and compliant to our *Cornerstones* and *Constitutional Foundation. We* must demand transparency (including governmental leader's private investments both during and after office), inspecting their actions and all expenditures. State and Federal leaders at all levels must be held responsible for failing to properly budget, plan and execute. Committing funds beyond revenue should be illegal, and surplus for unforeseen acts of God commended. If *We the People* don't hold our leaders accountable, they will certainly mortgage our children's future for their own present glory. *We* must DEMAND and EXPECT accountability, leaving our children with a sound government, strong fiscal foundation and well-defined strategic plan for their future!

Corruption is pandemic, and the media controls the narrative. Our nation's politics and financial vision is being funneled through the media prism, displaying a false reality and projecting a game that only the "elite" can win. The wealthy scratch the back of the wealthy which includes media moguls and politicians. Establishing a non-partisan, unpurchaseable and unbiased Internal Audit force should be our nation's top priority. This will be a struggle as witnessed in the highly partisan debacles during the appointments of Attorney General William Barr and Supreme Court Justice Brett Kavanaugh. Congress and their biased media arm focused on destroying all that challenge their control.

It's my strong opinion that every senior political leader and those assigned to positions of financial authority should be regularly audited, as well as their close associates and family. They must be held to a higher standard with more stringent accountability for self-serving actions. A perfect example of corruption is Vice President Joseph Biden, his son Hunter Biden and the family associates as noted earlier. Corporations associated with political leaders should also be in our audit sites, with any/all corrupt corporations being heavily fined for illegal efforts.

When leadership is held accountable, freedom is expanded, and growth is inevitable. We need a revised & long-term *Contract with America -* **ASAP!**

Chapter 20 – Our Nation's Infrastructure

In a storm at sea no one on board can wish the ship to sink, and yet not unfrequently all go down together because too many will direct, and no single mind can be allowed to control. Abraham Lincoln

If national pride is ever justifiable or excusable it is when it springs, not from power or riches, grandeur or glory, but from conviction of national innocence, information, and benevolence. John Adam

Go up to the hills and bring wood and build the house, that I may take pleasure in it and that I may be glorified, says the Lord. Haggai 1:8, ESV

~~~~~

Article I, Section 8.1 of our Constitution says: C*ongress has the Power To lay and collect Taxes, Duties, Imposts and Excises uniformly throughout the nation.* Article-IV, Section 4: *guarantees every State in this Union a Republican Form of Government, and protection against Invasion and domestic Violence"* (my summary).

Taxes are the means whereby we attain *"a more perfect Union, establish Justice, insure domestic Tranquility, provide for the common defence, promote the general Welfare, and secure the Blessings of Liberty to ourselves and our Posterity"*. This includes taxation by the separate states, counties, cities, townships and other incorporated communities. None should complain about paying taxes, but all should be concerned that our taxes are used wisely.

Along with a good National Defense/Offence, having a secure, safe and sound Infrastructure within our borders is essential to our nation's longevity on the Earth. As our several communities act on their own capitalistic and/or commonwealth enterprise, they in-turn enhance our national strength, curtailing weakness, expanding enterprise and ensuring our overall national security.

As a Capitalistic Republic, every community (local, state and territory) determines its own value and success. Communities that encourage growth and opportunity will attract more successful taxpayers, while communities that don't will and should fail. Just like an individual investing his/her *talent* to gain a return on investment, success has reward, but hiding or misusing talents (revenue) at every level doe and should end in loss.

This is what makes America unique and has kept America great. When an individual, company or community has value, all are blessed. When they take without giving, they fail. When individuals and communities aren't held accountable for their actions and depend on others to bail them out, then all fail. This is the destructive platform of Socialism/Communism.

An example of Capitalistic success/failure is the common church. If a church offers hope and comfort to its congregation then the tithes are gladly offered, and the church thrives. If the church fails to adequately minister to its congregation, tithes shrink, and the ministry diminishes. Imagine how things would be if the "state" were to choose winning churches and losing churches (which occurs in Socialist/Communist nations). If a church promotes what the political body says and receives funds taken by the governing body, then religious freedom is destroyed. Faith and hope will quickly be replaced with indoctrination and control.

 As states "compete" for quality taxpayers (individual and corporate), the need to provide a safe and pleasant environment is also essential for drawing in the best. Untainted competition enables government managers to enhance their infrastructures through increased revenues, resulting in greater opportunities and a more secure and comfortable citizenry. The Capitalistic society always wins if external meddling is avoided. Poor financial management at any level is a weakness, and external involvement results in enslavement.

America's Infrastructure has a rating of D+ according to the American Society of Civil Engineers (ASCE), revealing a lack of responsibility at the State and Federal levels. Aviation (D), Bridges (C+), Dams (D), Drinking Water (D), Electricity (D+), Energy (D+), Hazardous waste (D+), Inland Waterways (D), Levees (D), Parks (D+), Mass transit (D-), Ports (C+), Public spaces, Rail (B), Roads (D), Schools (D+),Solid waste (C+), Transportation (D-), Wastewater (D+).

The Council on Foreign Relations (CFR) estimated that our failing rail, road and waterways alone cause a loss of $billions in economic productivity each year. It's obvious that each category above affects our national health, welfare and security. Each are a critical aspect to our nation's defense, enjoyment and future. Political greed and a lack of understanding of these subjects and their relationship to enterprise have left our nation in a vulnerable and dire situation.

Our nation's most vulnerable infrastructure asset is our Border Security. Our borders are being continually violated resulting in the most egregious safety/security risk for our nation. Such occurs entirely due to the corruption of a powerful few in Congress and our Courts. A secure and controlled border system would save $billions if not $trillions in taxpayer monies currently wasted on battles against illicit drugs, human trafficking and the hand-outs for a select slave populace of illegal aliens. Such funds could enhance our National Defense posture as well as our vulnerable and unsafe infrastructure.

A critical national asset is the Information Technology, Data & Communications Infrastructure (ITDCI). Some of the objectives being assessed at the National Institute of Standards and Technology (NIST) include: Advanced Communications, Artificial Intelligence, Bioscience, Buildings and Construction, Chemistry, Cybersecurity, Electronics, Energy, Environment, Fire, Forensic Science, Health, Information technology, Infrastructure, Manufacturing, Materials, Mathematics and Statistics, Metrology, Nanotechnology, Neutron research, Performance Excellence, Physics, Public safety, Resilience, Standards, Transportation.

Though not quite as visible in its failure as a dam or bridge, nearly every major system within our nation is dependent on ITDCI, establishing it as one of our most important resources. Cyber security, Bioscience and Artificial Intelligence have become critical assets for any nation as well as a target for every enemy. Neglecting these strategic capabilities is detrimental to our nation.

If more young entrepreneurs and thinkers had better venues into the ITDCI arena, I'm certain that this critical infrastructure initiative could significantly improve. This one area is extremely critical and deserves extensive government control and accountability. Deterring our enemies from any attacks on our infrastructure and security should be our nation's top priority.

Except for ITDCI, most of our Infrastructure programs should be outsourced to the state or local levels for contracting to the most local level corporate ventures while maintaining auditable oversight. Lawmakers at both the Federal and State levels must be externally monitored for corruption and bias. All aspects of government and contract development within the ITDCI and media infrastructure must have the highest level of security and most stringent level of scrutiny.

Obviously, political leaders in both parties have long had their hand on the *corporate benefactor scale,* promoting their own political and financial agenda over the benefits of our nation. **Pay to play** is an abomination within our nation that must cease. Honest individual and corporate success are a blessing while political manipulation is always a curse. Uneven scales result in mistrust and diminished investment, greater political manipulation and vice.

America certainly needs more stringent laws and law enforcement against corrupt monopolies, the extremely wealthy and the politically powerful. Any who can control the people through the media, education system and governing laws must be controlled by *We the People*, while still promoting opportunities for success in these arenas. We must scrutinize the Federal Trade Commission, Federal Telecommunications Commission and our U. S. Treasury. None should be able to manipulate the market or our laws except by providing a better mousetrap at a reasonable price.

As Samuel Adams said, *"While the people are virtuous they cannot be subdued; but when once they lose their virtue, they will be ready to surrender their liberties to the first external or internal invader."* Add that to Tocqueville's *"The American Republic will endure until the day Congress discovers that it can bribe the public with the public's money"* concept, and you see the depravity of our political, media and wealthy elite.

Chapter 21 – Save the Planet

I like the dreams of the future better than the history of the past.
Thomas Jefferson

And God said, Let us make man in our image, after our likeness: and let them have dominion over the fish of the sea, and over the fowl of the air, and over the cattle, and over all the earth, and over every creeping thing that creepeth upon the earth. Genesis 1:26-28, KJV

He hath made every [thing] beautiful in his time: also he hath set the world in their heart, so that no man can find out the work that God maketh from the beginning to the end. Eccles 3:11, KJV

~~~~~

The end is near! Jesus is coming! Acid Rain! We're living in perilous times! The sky is falling!

Books, movies and scientific dissertations about the *end of the world* are selling like hotcakes! The world's end has been news since Christ walked the Earth based on scriptural prophesies about man's destructive nature, though many have falsely predicted the wrong date/time. Scientists and scholars have also predicted the Earth's destruction based on man's improper management of technological advances.

The *COVID panic of 2020* is a perfect example of how easily humans are manipulated by fear and how difficult it is to regain control when the media and government continue to promote a fear.

Since early on scholars and scientist have been selling us on the concept of the inevitable doom of man, from asteroids crashing to the Earth, our Sun either dying or going Nova, and even Extraterrestrials destroying our planet because of our evils. Since the 1300's, predictions by the religious, scientists, astronomers, astrologists and climatologists have said the end is near! Prestigious prophets like Nostradamus, Christopher Columbus, Martin Luther, the Mayan Calendar, Brahma Kumaris and Charles Manson (in Helter-Skelter) have suggested that man's end was long overdue.

The concept of "selling" was not a misworded term. Christians have used the *end of times* concept to scare the sinful to repentance, while scientists, astrologists and writers have been using the doomsday threat to garner a following and to sell their *visions* to the fearful. Books and movies harvest $billions from the fearful audience while scientists seek fame and fortune for their prophetic wisdom. Entrepreneurs rake in $billions more from the worrisome by selling fallout shelters, dried foods, weapons, ammo and the stockpiling of gold & silver. Humans are attracted to fear and a cause like flies are to... well, pretty much anything that stinks.

One of the most amazing prophesies of Scripture is found in Revelation chapter 9 which I read for the first time while stationed at MCB Camp Pendleton with the Marines, while literally sitting on a hill watching a training exercise play out in the valley below. In this chapter, the Apostle John foresees what I believe to be helicopters that resemble locusts from the pit with *faces of men, hair of women, crowns of gold, and the sound of chariots being pulled by horses into battle*. It was an eerie sight watching these green metal "grasshoppers" descend into the valley with turbo props whirling and destroying everything and "with a tail that stings" (their Scorpion Missiles). It certainly made me take notice as I considered my relationship with God in the 70's.

With that, I do believe that the nuclear, biological and chemical (NBC) developments of mankind have brought us to a place where we can easily destroy life as we know it. I'm certain that everyone reading this book has a continual fear of a nuclear attack and restitution from anywhere and everywhere, so yes, we can honestly say that man can now annihilate himself from the face of Earth. From another perspective, an asteroid (predicted for centuries) or significant heavenly event could also devastate our planet and even our Solar System. The evils of mankind are somewhat controllable, whereas the *acts of God* are certainly not.

Now I for one am a huge fan of caring for this planet we call home and am confident that most others feel the same. We love fresh air, clean water and beautiful lands. Even within our concrete jungles, we cherish our parks and green spaces, with businesses and communities continually seeking less invasive means to better our environment. It's just sensible. Then why is it that so many have such a hate against their fellow man for what we're doing? Our "G-XX" Summits and other global meetings where the leaders and speakers fly in on their jets, ride in their gas guzzling limousines, and then demean others for pollution is a sham! Follow the money! Like authors, speakers, film producers and politicians, making money and garnering votes from the fears of others is the oldest financial and political tactic in the book and just another form to enslave the masses.

Scientists research, analyze and summarize mounds of information seeking some new and exciting discovery that would affirm their theory. They look at the minutest of details, usually in some boring laboratory or office, just to discover something grand that they can put their name to (like a star). In general, there's nothing wrong with this intent, unless the intent is self-serving and meant to leverage the fears of others for personal or political gain or notoriety.

Dr. Peter Venkman (*Ghostbusters movie*) reveals this truth with humor as he tests for the 6th sense using cards and two human test cases - one being a nerdy guy and the other being a beautiful gal. As Venkman holds a card, he asks his volunteers to use their 6th sense to guess the graphic on the hidden side of a card. Of course, the beauty gets them all "correct" while the nerdy guy gets shocked for unwittingly having the wrong answers (with Venkman never revealing the truth of the cards). The real study was obviously a test of Venkman's gravitational pull on the heart of the beauty!

Fifty years ago, Wisconsin Democratic Senator Gaylord Nelson shook the world and caused generation after generation to fear the extinction of man with the first *Earth Day*. Infamous sales-pitches were reported around the world that unnerved millions through his lies:

- "In a decade, urban dwellers will have to wear gas masks to survive air pollution…",

- "By 1985 air pollution will have reduced the amount of sunlight reaching earth by one half….",

- "At the present rate of nitrogen buildup, it's only a matter of time before light will be filtered out of the atmosphere and none of our land will be usable."(Ecologist Kenneth Watt),

- "Civilization will end within 15 or 30 years unless immediate action is taken against problems facing mankind." (Harvard biologist George Wald),

- "The death rate will increase until at least 100-200 million people per year will be starving to death during the next ten years." (Biologist Paul Ehrlich),

- "We are in an environmental crisis which threatens the survival of this nation, and of the world as a suitable place of humans". (Denis Hayes, Chief organizer, Earth Day),

None of these predictions came to pass, nor did the world's end as predicted by Johannes Stöffler's World Flood in 1524, Rigiomontanus in 1588, Haley's Comet Collision of 1910, Martin Luther's prediction of 1600 or the Mayan Calendar Prediction for 2012. NASA data shows a period of warming in the 1920's and 30's, followed by two or three decades of cooling temperatures. At that time many experts, including Carl Sagan, warned us of a possible Ice Age, only to have the climate change on them, again. From the 1970s to the late 1990s, scientists began to record slightly warmer temperatures which was confirmed when NASA sounded the alarm for "Global Warming". A short time later the New York Times cited the National Oceanic and Atmospheric Administration (NOAA) data as showing no warming over the past 100 years in the U. S. at all!

Obviously, something's amiss within our scientific studies and historical readings. None have died from Climate Change though millions of people and thousands of businesses have been destroyed by the fears of such theory and the government sanctions predicated on such lies. The predictions of Earth Day were typical manipulation tactics used against the masses for a political agenda, as we saw an an opposing reality play out. Why is it that the U.N. and many national leaders promote and act upon a Global Crisis? Follow the money!

Former VP Al Gore, worth an estimated $300 million, is one of those who promoted the evils of man and fossil fuels while flying around in his private jets promoting **his** alternatives, concepts and businesses. Interestingly, he's also a proponent for murdering millions of babies in America each year, so it's obvious that he doesn't care about humanity.

Allow me to share my thoughts on how we save our planet! **First**, we must accept that we are all one family of humans meant to fit together as a team. **Second**, we must end the manipulating and gaming of the people's fears and emotions. **Third**, we must seek to better understand the perfection of *Creation* and how we can best fit within it using the least invasive means (yes, environmentally conscious). **Fourth**, we should work desperately to deter and diminish weapons of mass destruction (WMD) around the globe. **Fifth,** we must focus on our ability to heal instead of attack and rescue instead of condemning.

Though a few at the top seem to hold all the cards, we've each been created to secure *Life, Liberty* and the ability to *Pursue* to honor one another and to care for our planet. *Acts of God* can alter or destroy life as we know it through a diminishing Sun or asteroid hit while man can also alter or destroy life as we know it. If mankind genuinely accepts that Earth and all that's in it as a perfect design and puts the whole above his own selfish desires, then his talents can be used to better care for ourselves, our planet and our future. We could even redirect our resources towards potential *acts of God* such as an asteroid strike or other global catastrophe. There's a reason that we have been endowed with these abilities, and if we work together instead of against one another for selfish gain, we can survive and thrive.

So, all exists on purpose and for a purpose, and I'd take this to the extent that all things are created in a way that seeks to reestablish the presumptive Garden of Eden. It's the human acts of controlling others (Socialism, Communism, Dictatorship) that diminish man's abilities to pursue and implement what is good and right. Technologies and programs can certainly be used to attack and destroy, though these same technologies can be used to rescue and heal. Technology is good, but it has consequences. Technology creates wealth, as seen by Facebook and Amazon, but it can also destroy all if used to divide and conquer.

We must fight the evil force that desires to *steal, kill and destroy*. To do so, we must focus instead on how we can expand our understanding of the *Creator*, His creation, the *life* He has given, the *liberty* He has established, and the ability to *pursue happiness* that He has promised!

Chapter 22 – Zombies in America

We live, my dear soul, in an age of trial. What will be the consequences, I know not. President John Adams

You never know how much you really believe anything until its truth or falsehood becomes a matter of life and death to you. C. S. Lewis

Yea, though I walk through the valley of the shadow of death, I will fear no evil: for thou art with me; thy rod and thy staff they comfort me. Psalm 23:4, KJV

Whoever claims to love God yet hates a brother or sister is a liar. For whoever does not love their brother and sister, whom they have seen, cannot love God, whom they have not seen. 1 John 4:20, NIV

~~~~~

We are overrun with *zombies*! "Dead people" are walking through life, seeking to take the life of others…

With the many predictions of our planet's doom by asteroid, nuclear war, or destruction through pollution, what difference would it make if existence is an accident? Those who deny a Creator and promote existence as chance and science alone (Evolutionists), can't truly believe that existence was from an accidental *Big Bang*, or why would they care about their own family or anything else for that matter? If life ends at death, what would anything matter? Live and take all you can, should be their lifestyle!

Two thousand years ago in a letter to a new church in Ephesus, the Apostle Paul wrote an amazing word of warning:

> *"And you were **dead** in the trespasses and sins in which you once walked, following the course of this world, following the prince of the power of the air, the spirit that is now at work in the sons of disobedience— among whom we all once lived in the passions of our flesh, carrying out the desires of the body and*

*the mind, and were by nature **children of wrath**, like the rest of mankind."* (Eph 2:1-3, ESV).

Abraham likely knew his great-great-Grandpa Noah and his sea-faring family. Hearing directly from Noah and the others of their Ark stories and the millions who died during the flood, probably put great fear into Abraham's heart of this all-powerful Creator. It always amazes me that the Vedic (pre-Hindu) God called *Indra* (the likely religion of Abram's family) the God of *"creation, heaven, storms and flooding"*. Coincidence? I think not. Anyway, Abraham became a very devout and faithful man who *God* called to leave his home in Mesopotamia and head to the Mediterranean coast to establish his families (Hebrews, Ishmaelites, Arabs Tribes and Christians).

Abraham's grandson Jacob (Israel) had his 11th son Joseph, who was sold by his brothers into slavery in Egypt. After properly explaining and interpreting Pharaoh's dream of an impending famine, Joseph was appointed as leader over all of Egypt. His policies then rescued millions from the famine including his own family (father, brother and all) who had relocated to Egypt. Over the next 400 or so years, the Israelites grew in number and were forced into slavery by the Egyptians. God then calls Moses (a Jewish boy raised in Pharaoh's house) to deliver the Israelites out of Egypt, through ten plagues that show His power. The final plague kills all the firstborn throughout Egypt (human and animal) while the Hebrews (Israelites) are spared.

For death to *"Passover"* the children of Israel, God had them strike the top and sides of their doors with the blood of an unblemished (perfect) male lamb. Death comes to all the first born in Egypt, while passing over the houses of the Israelites and any who place the blood on their door posts. Pharaoh finally relents and sends Moses and the Israelites (estimated at 3,000,000 people) away, who eventually return to the land promised to Abraham for his family, which is today's Israel.

Over the next 1500 years, the Jews celebrate the *Passover*, sacrificing a perfect lamb for the sins of the nation. Throughout that time, various Prophets tell of another deliverer like Moses who would bring eternal freedom and power to the His "chosen people", calling him the "Mashiach ben David" (Messiah, son of David), revealing prophetic details of this coming Messiah.

> *"For to us a child is born, to us a son is given, and the government will be on his shoulders. And he will be called Wonderful Counselor, Mighty God, Everlasting Father, Prince of Peace."* (Isaiah 9:6, NIV).

Yet it was our weaknesses he carried; it was our sorrows that weighed him down. And we thought his troubles were a punishment from God, a punishment for his own sins! But he was pierced for our rebellion, crushed for our sins. He was beaten so we could be whole. He was whipped so we could be healed.

But it was the LORD's good plan to crush him and cause him grief. Yet when his life is made an offering for sin, he will have many descendants. He will enjoy a long life, and the LORD's good plan will prosper in his hands." (Isaiah 53:4-5 & 10, NLT).

Christians believe that Jesus was this Messiah, born of the virgin Mary in Bethlehem who at 30 years old began his ministry of healing, raising people from the dead and preaching the news of salvation and life after death. After 3 years of ministry, the Hebrew Priests and Roman Governor (Pilate), tried, flogged and crucified Jesus on the cross - **on the Passover**. According to His followers, Jesus rose from the grave and was seen by them for 40 days afterward before being taken-up into heaven, with a promise by Angels nearby that He would return in the same way. Jesus' disciples, who had abandoned him during His trial, after seeing Him alive again 3 days later and over the following 40 days, gave their very lives to preach redemption for all through His sacrifice and resurrection.

Saul (renamed Paul), was a very zealous young Jewish priest, sent by the Jewish leaders to capture and destroy the growing followers of Jesus. On his way to persecute believers (called Christians), he was confronted by a vision of Jesus and given revelation about the Messiah. Paul then spent the remaining days sharing news of eternal life before being beheaded by Emperor Nero in Rome for his faith.

One of Paul's companions during his 30-year mission work was Luke, the author of the Gospel of his own name. Luke shares the popular Christmas accounts we hear each year about Jesus' birth. As a Roman physician and historian Luke was certainly not one to embellish or create fictitious stories. His accounts of Christ's birth and early life were more detailed than the other Gospel writers, suggesting that he (and probably Paul) likely spent time with Jesus' mother Mary and/or his sisters & brothers, in order to gain such details confirming that Jesus fulfilled the prophesies of the Messiah, ***the Lamb of God.***

Again, the 700-year-old prophesy by Isaiah said it best, *"But he was pierced for our rebellion, crushed for our sins. He was beaten so we could be whole."* As a Jewish Rabbi and religious zealot, Paul knew the Jewish Scriptures and doctrines better than most. He also knew of man's evil nature and God's judgement on those who were evil, including the chosen family of Israel. His conclusion was that all are dead in their sins… **Zombies!**

If there is an *Adversary* of the *Creator*, he/it would certainly be an adversary of *creation*, and especially those created in the *Creator's* image (mankind). Since none are perfect or qualified for heaven, there is a need for a perfect and pure sacrifice to *"take away the sins of the world"* (John 1:29, NIV). Nearly 2,000 years before Jesus, Abraham told his son Isaac that *"God will provide himself a lamb for the burnt offering…"* (Gen 22:8, KJV). Little did he know, the Lamb would be his own descendent.

So Paul tells the new church in Ephesus, *"And you were dead in the trespasses and sins, in which you once walked, following the course of this world, following the prince of the power of the air, the spirit that is now at work in the sons of disobedience."* Yep, they were all the **walking dead** following the *Dark Side.* But then he says this:

> *"But God, being rich in mercy, because of the great love with which he loved us, even when we were **dead** in our trespasses, made us **alive** together with Christ—by grace you have been saved…"* (Eph 2:1-5, ESV).

Christ's sacrifice and resurrection were for all of mankind from every religion and people. Though none know all truth or what comes after this life (I'm confident there's something), it seems that we are most certainly created on purpose and for a purpose. If you haven't, I'd strongly recommend reading the Bible (Old and New Testaments) without the influence of anyone else. Start with the New Testament and then go back to Genesis, Exodus and the Chronicles. Mind you, it's about Christ's sacrifice for our eternal life while being a *Human Users-Manual* to help us to better understand our life and purpose.

-**Hinduism** reveals a God of creation, life and eternity
-**Judaism** reveals the timeline of man and the laws of God
-**Islam** reveals the judgement of God on those who forsake Him
-**Christianity** reveals the grace of God for those who seek Him

Chapter 23 – Pursuit of Happiness

The purpose of life is not to be happy. It is to be useful, to be honorable, to be compassionate, to have it make some difference that you have lived and lived well. Ralph Waldo Emerson

I the Lord search the heart and test the mind, to give every man according to his ways, according to the fruit of his deeds. Jeremiah 17:10, ESV

Greater love has no one than this: to lay down one's life for one's friends. John 15:13, NIV

~~~~~

It's my opinion that much like the Walking Dead programs on TV and in theater, we are all being pursued by those seeking to make us as they are, *zombies*!

Evidence throughout nature, literature and historical accounts all seem to point towards the plight of overcoming our own selfish *zombie* nature. Then, as we heal within ourselves, we then must battle the *zombies* whose intent is to destroy our freedoms, our lives, and the lives of those we love. In John's Gospel, he records the account of a Jewish leader (Nicodemus) who secretly came to Jesus one evening after seeing the miracles that Jesus did. Before he even asks a question, Jesus says, *"I tell you the truth, unless you are born again, you cannot see the Kingdom of God."* (John 3:3, NLT).

I doubt anyone fully understand what being *born again* or the *Kingdom of God* mean, but Jesus goes on to tell the Jewish leader that famous quote: *"For this is how God loved the world: He gave his one and only Son, so that everyone who believes in him will not perish but have eternal life. God sent his Son into the world not to judge the world, but to save the world through him."* (John 3:16-17, NLT).

My interpretation – humans have the sentence of death on them at birth by our inherent selfish and evil choices, making us all *zombies* in need of a cure. The cure offered was the blood of God's own sacrifice with His death in place of ours if we accept his forgiveness. According to Scripture, this new life is for both this life as well as an eternal life beyond. Obviously, none know exactly what that will be like, nor can any prove this concept, but somehow it makes sense.

The H. O. P. E. Rose (Wilson)

Earlier, I shared the concept of the *H.O.P.E. Rose* that points the stumbling zombies of this planet towards the *World's Greatest Treasure* – their heart (the **Desire** Compass Point). Sadly, but all too often, extreme challenges from the hands of others can alter a person's balance, establishing *F.E.A.R.* as the primary guidance, with *H.O.P.E.* being more of a mockery to their hurting souls.

All animals adapt to their environment, and we humans are not an exception to such adaptation. Our early environments of being no-mads, and then creating farms, homesteads and eventually cities as our communities expand is only natural. Whether in the mountains, at the beach or in the city, encouraging, abusive and even absent families mold us into who we will become. Being raised in an off-balance world where fright, extreme emotions, anxiety and regret (condemnation) are the norm will naturally guide us towards a similarly imbalance future. Sometimes though, humans catch a glimmer of truth and hope, breaking free from their native state. We often write about such people as overcomers and champions, and most of our greatest novels and movies are founded on this principle.

The words of the old slave trader John Newton (1725–1807) said it best, *"Amazing Grace, how sweet the sound that saved a wretch like me; I once was lost but now am found, was blind but now I see.".* As the captain of a Slave Ship, John caught the glimmer of hope and traded his chains for grace, fighting to end the slave trade around the globe. As I searched for truth, I had a choice during an illness of either reading a smut magazine (for the 10th or so time) or a small New Testament. I opted for the New Testament, and it captured my heart. Something in me knew there was more, and I believe this book is it.

It's my belief that being *born-again* enables us to relinquish our roots of following *F.E.A.R.,* giving us the opportunity to pursue *H.O.P.E.* and purpose while still living in this *zombie* world. This is the *True North* of all great doctrines and writings throughout history and within all religions, even those that do not acknowledge Jesus or His purpose. Yet Scripture says that He died for all (done deal), and not a specific group, sect, religion, race or other category of human. ALL can be healed from their life as a Zombie to live a life of purpose and honor.

Using Paul as an example, we don't know what we don't know until we "see the light". We may fight and condemn what is right (Paul's mission was to persecute Christians) without knowing that it's our escape from a road that's going in the wrong direction. We are all brought into this world by imperfect parents, raised in an imperfect house, have imperfect friends and are taught by imperfect teachers. How can we possibly know what's right? Even when things seem perfect, I can guarantee you that all are dysfunctional. As Scripture says, *"No one is righteous— not even one".* (Rom 3:10, NLT).

The coddled become spoiled and demanding, the abused become angry and self-destructive, while the misguided become wanderers seeking rogue trails, validation and revenge. All who have been or may presently be enslaved, threatened or abused can accept the forgiveness of the *Creator* and leverage their unique abilities, skills and background into talents that can honor others. Like a coin (talent) that takes a precious metal, melted by heat and then molded by its creator to establish something of value and worth. We have all been given the opportunity to escape the land of the *zombies* and to use our designed talent for not just personal gain but gain that is meant to extend beyond our life. I doubt any really know what that is exactly, but I believe the *Creator* does and that His design for you is immeasurable and priceless.

Chapter 24 – Our Nation's Compass

"From the day of the Declaration... They (the American people) were bound by the laws of God, which they all, and by the laws of The Gospel, which they nearly all, acknowledge as the rules of their conduct." - John Quincy Adams

If you have a chance to accomplish something that will make things better for people coming behind you, and you don't do that, you are wasting your time on this earth. Roberto Clemente

Make me know Your ways, O LORD; Teach me Your paths. Lead me in Your truth and teach me, For You are the God of my salvation; For You I wait all the day. Psalms 25:4-5, KJV

I lift up my eyes to the mountains-- where does my help come from? My help comes from the LORD, the Maker of heaven and earth. Psalms 121:1-2, NIV

~~~~~

Forbes Magazine recently published an article by senior contributor Kathy Caprino about the **"Top 8 Things People Desperately Desire but Can't Seem to Attain"**:

1. *Happiness*: Not knowing what I want to do.
2. *Money*: Adequate time & money to do what I want
3. *Freedom*: Having the freedom to find my "true purpose"
4. *Peace*: Having clarity about who I am and my purpose
5. *Joy*: Finding the right role or position that will bring joy in my work
6. *Balance*: Balancing needs, desires, flexibility, money & benefits
7. *Fulfillment*: Best utilizing my potential for self and others
8. *Confidence*: Having something to offer today and as I am

I'm sure you can relate to Kathy's list, and would likely claim the same top-8, though maybe in a different order. Sadly, Kathy identified that these desires are mostly unattainable, yet I'd suggest that if we properly employ the *Compass points* of **H.O.P.E.** and **F.E.A.R.**, all can attain their **Desperate Desires**. Notice too that in the descriptions of each, the foundational aspect is **Purpose**, or the implementation of our **Talents through action!**

We as humans desire purpose and value in life, which in turn provides *confidence, fulfillment, joy, financial satisfaction* and *happiness*. The two **Desires** that stand-out in Kathy's list to me are **Freedom** and **Balance**. As *unique* **individuals** we have *unique* **Talents** whereby **Freedom** enables us to **Balance** our lives and empower our **Purpose**. Imbalance comes from being forced into a government-controlled environment where none are unique or special, and all are simply used as the "superiors" deem best.

I recently had the privilege of seeing Vice President Mike Pence at the CPAC-2020 Conference in Washington, DC., and hearing his message of hope for our nation; hope to save the lives of our unborn and born, hope for our economy and hope for a future. His words were words of honor and optimism for all Americans as well as the peoples of other nations around the globe. VP Pence also humbly and properly addressed concerns that our nation's *Cornerstones* and *Foundation* are being attacked in an open affront to destroy our *freedom* and *balance.*

It's undeniable that our Constitution, Declaration and Laws are under attack by the same enemy of our nation that pushed to expand slavery some 200 years ago. This enemy today, portrays a false veneer of compassion in order to establish their political control, desiring nothing more than to expand the slavery plantation beyond the Black and Latino communities. To accomplish this, they must first abolish our individual uniqueness, freedom and purpose, and establish a controlled environment for all, discounting individual purpose. This is the intent of the Democratic Socialist platform we see today, with their motto being "No Trump, No Wall, No U.S.A. at all!"

- Winston Churchill - *The inherent vice of capitalism is the unequal sharing of blessings; the inherent virtue of socialism is the equal sharing of miseries.*

- Bernie Sanders - *Democratic socialism means that we must reform a political system that is corrupt, that we must create an economy that works for all, not just the very wealthy.*

- Karl Marx - *Democracy is the road to socialism.*

- Vladimir Lenin - *The goal of socialism is communism.*

The quotes above have played-true since *Marx & Engels* first defined their *revolutionary* intent in their *Communist Manifesto*. As noted by Sir Winston Churchill, capitalism is the personification of *Jesus' Parable of the Talents*, with each human receiving talents and purposes designed to create a Return on Investment (ROI). Those who invest their talents receive their *Desires*, while those who hide their talent (deceivers) struggle to find their purpose, balance and *Desires*. In a society founded on God, Life, Liberty and Pursuit, all have the skill to create, provide and receive without government bias. When a government controls it's people (slaves), all lose their liberty and ability to pursue.

Rudolph Joseph Rummel (Died in 2014), was a professor of political science at the Universities of Indiana, Yale and Hawaii who spent his career studying violence and war in the 1900's. He estimated that 150 million citizens were killed by Communist governments such as the Stalinist purges and Mao's Cultural Revolution. As noted by Lenin, Socialism by intent becomes Communism to control or eliminate opposition. Rummel coined the term *democide* for such murders by government.

An example is the order by Stalin to "liquidate" the class of Russians called 'kulaks' (peasants with two cows or five/six acres more than their neighbors). This liquidation is believed to have caused the Soviet famine of 1932–1933. Terms accredited to the Socialist/Communist takeovers include *Genocide* (ethnic killings), *Politicide* (political killings), *Democide* (unarmed opponent killings), *Classicide* (Class killings), and *Holocausts* (massive killings with any intent). Though Rummel claimed that the death of the 150 million peasants as murder, most historians avoid such a term in order to hide this protocol of Socialist takeovers. It's believed that there were tens of millions more murdered than what has been officially recorded. When freedom and opportunity is stolen, war and death will follow.

Senator Bernie Sanders, Senator Chuck Schumer, Representative Nancy Pelosi and the overall Democratic Party are beginning to feel the pinch that their control over the American slave populace is weakening. As such, they have come out of the closet to proclaim their intent to overthrow this nation *of the people, by the people and for the people*, to establish a socialist rule whereby the few elites enslave the masses, just as Marx foretold.

I can hear you saying, "this will never happen"! However, our *"One nation under God, indivisible, with liberty and justice for all"* has legalized and funded the murder of nearly 70 million American babies in their mother's womb, in the name of "Choice". You can't tell me that the people willing to murder the most innocent wouldn't also murder the aged and affirmed on their path to their selfish desires. An example was the recent forced admission of COVID-19 patience into Nursing homes in California, New Jersey, New York, Pennsylvania and other Democrat run states around New England.

Surely, the Democratic Party that expanded the bloody blemish of slavery throughout the centuries has knowingly sacrificed all for their own personal gain. This Party that created the Ku Klux Klan, murdered millions of babies, enslaved millions within our slums/barrios and promotes sexual perversion, has now murdered hundreds if not thousands of our most vulnerable through regulated infections within their nursing homes. Truly reflective of Hitler, Lenin, Stalin, Mao and others whose intent was to steal, kill and destroy.

The coming 2020 elections will be a choice between death and slavery or a return to our Capitalistic and Republican standards. Freedom can only be restored by reestablishing of our Cornerstones, Constitution, and conscience of morality. We must ensure every American, from inception to grave, is supported by a free and balanced government that enables them to pursue their PURPOSE and achieve their DESIRES!

Chapter 25 – A Nation of Champions

If thou wouldst rule well, thou must rule for God, and to do that, thou must be ruled by Him... Those who will not be governed by God will be ruled by tyrants. William Penn

A hero is an ordinary individual who finds the strength to persevere and endure in spite of overwhelming obstacles. Christopher Reeve

We then that are strong ought to bear the infirmities of the weak, and not to please ourselves. Romans 15:1-2, KJV

I lift up my eyes to the mountains-- where does my help come from? My help comes from the LORD, the Maker of heaven and earth. Psalms 121:1-2, NIV

~~~~~

Our nation has been here before, with heroes rising from the masses to rescue her and usher in a global hope. As John Stuart Mills wrote, *"War is an ugly thing, but not the ugliest of things: the decayed and degraded state of moral and patriotic feeling which thinks that nothing is worth a war, is much worse."* It's my belief that a generation of freedom fighters are being groomed within our borders and around the globe that few recognize. Not an armed militia but a band of young heroes who desire truth and honor.

Today's newest generation has been enamored with movies of champions such as *The Avengers, American Sniper, Lord of the Rings, Harry Potter, The Hunger Games, Star Wars* and so many, many more. Though our theatres and televised media outlets push evil and perverted venues without pause, the huge success of our blockbuster hero movies are cause for hope. Yes, it's my earnest belief that as the *Dark Side* attempts to plant fear and hopelessness in the minds of our youth, we have more 13 to 30-year-old heroes in America today than at any other time in our nation's history. Young heroes urged on by the likes of Lee, Spielberg, Rawlings, Lucas and others, groomed for action with a heart to rescue the oppressed, defend the weak and free the slaves.

I'm amazed at how many young men go out of their way to talk to me about the SEAL Teams, being a sniper, the Marines and all sorts of heroic aspirations. Many of these aren't the physically powerful or SEAL/Marine type, but all have this same fire in their eyes! There's a call to be a hero, and a belief that technology and heart are the equalizing factor that will turn them from the intellectual geek type into a *Hulk* when the time is right.

Several young ladies have approached me as well with the same "fire" in their eyes, but with a more traditional concern and ambition, to make the world a better place for their future and their children's future. Fear over their hope to marry their best friend, have a family, and pursue their happiness is a constant concern. They feel the oppression of the enemy trying to destroy their dreams of a strong family and hope, yet many are confident that an army of heroes will rise within their peers, and side by side they will conquer the coming battle – though uncertainty remains!

The largest overlooked group are our young heroes in the inner city. The Slave Master's intent of division, confusion and animosity have created a downward spiral for most, as seen in previous charts, yet looking at the sports heroes of the day, these young warriors are focused and hardworking when a chance is presented. The 2018 American superhero film *Black Panther* by *Marvel and Walt Disney Studios* shows the real-world challenge that these future leaders are up against from those within their own community who desire to control and gain from their strengths.

Again, there's a political move to keep our young on the plantation (any nationality, color, religion or creed) and dependent upon the "candy man" or slave masters within their communities. These slave masters push an agenda of distrust of others who promote hope and escape. Divide and conquer has and always will be a powerful weapon of war, not only in politics (Alinsky's Principles and Communist Manifesto) but in combat as revealed in the 2,500-year-old work *The Art of War* by *Sun Tzu*. The principle is simple – identify a difference (any kind), incite hatred against it, and then capitalize on the emotions. Black/white, rich/poor, English/Spanish, tall/short, thin/fat, intellectual/physical, or any trait available. If all were the same except for eye color, an us-against-them scenario would be leveraged to ***divide, conquer & control***.

Here's another huge area of division that man and the Adversary of God uses against one another – Religion! As mentioned earlier, if we've all come from Noah, we're not only cousins but our religions all come from the same foundation. Reading the 1944 *Viking Press World Bible* Edited by Robert O. Ballou, I see a common theme/understanding – love and honor the Creator, love and honor our fellow man, and battle your selfish and evil ambitions. Since no two people are the same, no two people have the same beliefs either. I can assure you, even Noah believed differently from his wife, sons and daughters-in-law. Though our uniqueness gives us purpose, it's also the means whereby we're so easily manipulated and divided. Religion (belief of purpose) is certainly one of our most unique traits, and none can say that their beliefs are "truth", otherwise they're claiming to be all knowing, and they're not!

At the birth of Jesus, the Angel was sent to shepherds (the lowest of people), saying, *"Fear not: for I bring you good tidings of great joy, which shall be to **all people**"* (Luke 2:10, KJV), much like Jesus' statement to Nicodemus saying, *"whosoever believes"*. The Creator intentionally created all we know and intentionally created our uniqueness, allowing us the opportunity to experience temptation, sorrow, repentance, forgiveness, and conquest! Division is just the Adversary's way of diminishing our uniqueness, diverting our purpose and discrediting our successes.

This chapter is a battle cry for us older folks to take responsibility for the nation we're passing on to those who follow, suggesting we criticize less and encourage more. We should trust that life will provide our younger adults with opportunities to establish their unique talents, prove their worth, and seek a return on their investments. We should encourage their attempts to be different (unique), providing them an example of how to appreciate their uniqueness. Just like we struggled in our youth with finding our road, we must allow them to seek theirs as well. The key is to instill in their hearts the knowledge of the *Dark Side (Adversary)* intent to steal, kill and destroy, while providing them the platform of building on Life, Liberty and Pursuit. These young readily spot hypocrites, so we cannot be complacent.

Could we be in the *"end times"*? Certainly. Jesus said – *"as the days of Noah were, so also will the coming of the Son of Man be."* (Matt 24:37, NKJV). Remember that before the flood, all but 8 were eating, drinking and marrying, expecting life to go on as always. As suggested, it's my belief that mankind was at least as *advanced* as we are today, though probably in different ways than we can even fathom but may be revealed as we better understand the pyramids and such. But their selfish and evil ways were their own demise.

Scripture (Old and New Testament) reveals that the next global catastrophe will be by fire from the skies, attacks from flying craft and the destruction of our natural resources (Ezekiel 38 and 39 / Revelations 9). The Disciple John even foresaw 200,000,000 calvary troops ascending on Israel, and the destruction of 1/3 of the people, waters and living creatures (Revelation 9), while the entire population at the time of his writing may not have reached that. Interestingly, China boasted in the 60's of having a marching army 200 million strong (Time Magazine), and the anti-Israel Muslim coalition has claimed they too have an army of 200 million. Though I've discarded the fear of Climate Change as the world's demise, we must acknowledge that a nuclear disaster is a mere button click away. The hands being played at the gambling table are not gambling with money but with the future of mankind and the world.

Though I periodically worry about end-time prophesies, I identify it as being beyond my control except to pray over. My hope is that Providence will continue to deal the cards in a way that doesn't destroy mankind but rescues it so my children's children for generations to come will have the same opportunities to learn to love and overcome as we have. For my part, I will continue to work on making our world a safer, more productive and more hopeful, though at times such a hope is hard to see, and I'd almost pray for heavenly fire to destroy those who practice evil. Still, I will work to do my part to pray for expanded life, liberty and happiness, to thwart the enemy's plan to steal, kill and destroy, and to free the people under the enemy's control.

Though disaster is more intriguing, there's another prophesy in the book of Revelation (chapter 20) that is less talked about - where peace reigns for a thousand years. Like the other prophesies of scripture, I can't prove times or sequences, but I like this thought of hope and peace, and would prefer to press for this to occur more than the 1/3 destruction of mankind and the Earth. As Jesus said, none would know the day or hour, but in my opinion, it's our task to pursue *Hope, Opportunity, Purpose and Enthusiasm* using the compass of *Desire* as our guide and to teach such to our young.

The hand we've been dealt has two basic players: those who play an honest hand of *compassion* and *hope,* and those who bluff with *compassion while intent on capture and control*! It's my opinion that the *Trump Card* has been played to reveal the hearts of men and women around the globe, and specifically within our nations leadership.

Chapter 26 – It's Our Play

"From the day of the Declaration...they (the American people) were bound by the laws of God, which they all, and by the laws of The Gospel, which they nearly all, acknowledge as the rules of their conduct." - John Quincy Adams

Beloved, I pray that in all respects you may prosper and be in good health, just as your soul prospers. 3 John 1:2, NAS

~~~~~

It's obvious that our nation's foundation is vulnerable, and Americans are fearful and weak. The COVID lockdown and the subsequent Economic shutdown are examples of how easily the masses can be manipulated. Our Republic, the U.S. Constitution (U.S.C.) and our laws were established to protect us from such government overreach. We must survive this season of panic, elect a *pro-Constitutional Congress,* and reset our *Cornerstones.* The following lists what I believe America must do to remove the noose around her neck that has been tightening throughout the last 150 years:

A Religious Republic

Our first play must be to reaffirm Biblical principles and a relationship between our *Government, Education System and Providence*. In our Republic, all of *Life, Liberty and Property* must be protected as **unalienable rights**. Religion/faith is the most important "property" humans can possess and as such must be encouraged and protected for all. Freedom from Religion is not Freedom, and there is no *Constitutional* or legal provision for *Separation of Church and State.*

The Sanctity of Life

As one nation under God, we must reaffirm the God-given legal personhood of all humans from fertilization to natural death without exception. Our *Declaration, Constitution, and* the *Creator* Himself demand protection of innocent life which no civil government should harm without justification. Infanticide and euthanasia must be outlawed!

Election Reform

Our nation's future relies upon valid voting practices. Federal level elections must be restricted to living and legal U. S. Citizens alone with adequate safeguards, monitoring, and audits at every poll ensuring authorization to vote one time per citizen. State elections must also comply with Citizenship standards and Federal/State laws ensuring legal and constitutional Electoral Representation.

Congressional Reform

Term Limits must be established for Congress members and staff by Act or Convention. Removing the opportunity to game the system for personal gain is a must. Fiscal perks (such as pensions) should be discontinued, and deep audits completed to deter corruption. Strong anti-corruption laws and assessments must be established for members of Congress and their immediate family during terms of service and subsequent 5 years.

An Act/Convention must also mandate an **on-time annual Balanced Budget** with strict penalties for failure to comply.

Judicial Reform

Justices have also become partisan tools of the Executive and Legislative Branches, promoting and allowing corruption within their chambers. It is therefore strongly recommended that Congress or a Convention of States pass **Term Limits** for all Judiciary members. (U. S. C. Article 3, Section 1)

Presidential Reform

The President of the United States represents *We the People* and as such, must be held to the highest standards but also must be defended against corrupt leaders and media attacks. U. S. C. Article 1 assigns the President as Commander in Chief of Military to establish global Treaties and to coordinate/appoint key public positions to promote America on the world stage. The President is our elected leader and must be respected.

Executive Orders must be constrained, precise and supported by Constitutional intentions and scrutinized by Congress and the Supreme Court as appropriate.

National Service Act (NSA)

Considering the precipice on which America stands, it is appropriate and necessary for the United States of America to establish a *National Service Act,* requiring every American citizen (age 17/18 – no exception) to serve their country in an elected/qualified field of service for two (2) years. This Act will extend Selective Service beyond National Defense to National Infrastructure (Police, Fire, Utilities, Parks, etc.), National Health Systems, International Humanitarian Service programs, Homeland Security, and similar initiatives. Every American must serve our nation!

The **NSA** will produce an immediate decrease in poverty, crime, drug addiction, racial division, and other challenges facing our youth and nation today. It will provide vocational training, financial knowledge, expanded awareness, and a pathway into further education and the professional capabilities of our future leaders. It will also benefit programs being served with fresh thoughts and energies from various backgrounds and experiences of our bold and powerful youth. Above all, it will offer each of our American citizens with hope and opportunity.

The **NSA** will necessitate a well-planned, funded and organized start-up strategy and execution. Many of our military, professional service and not-for-profit programs have extensive experience in such mentoring initiatives making execution plausible. Partnering with Federal, State, Corporate and Humanitarian leaders around the nation to establish this initiative would be readily achievable with an instant impact on American society and national strength.

As with our National Defense, service members will receive commensurate wages, room, board, health benefits and as such as appropriate. Upon completion of service, a benefit package would be provided that would support further education, entrance into the work force or extended opportunities to serve within the various programs. Again, the Selective Service program and military contracted services are an example and ready platform.

A 2/3 Majority of Congress plus Presidential Approval or Convention of States would be necessary to establish an NSA.

Federal Fiscal Responsibility

The Federal Government has repetitively used national crisis to unduly tax her Citizens, purchase votes and control the people. They have stolen from us for generations and have now placed a $23 trillion plus debt on our children's shoulders with no strategy to correct such corrupt practices. Congress and the President must be held accountable for their fiscal irresponsibility. If they can't create a balanced budget they should not be paid. Article 1, Section 6 provides for Compensation to members of Congress, yet such pay can be denied for "Treason, Felony and Breach of Peace" of which Congress has obviously succumbed.

Social Security is a questionable form of individual retirement that must remain solvent for those who depend on their lifetime investment. A "Volunteer Social Security Initiative" should be established that is untouchable by Congress but not mandated or socialized.

The Internal Revenue Service is corrupt and must be reorganized, reduced or discontinued altogether. Though taxation is appropriate and necessary, it must wholly support the security and safety of Americans alone and not be used as a "benefit" or "entitlement" fund. Though beyond the scope of this book, *Tax Reform* is critical to our nation's survival and must be made simple and consistent for all (poorest to wealthiest). Intentional complexities and specialized deductions are corrupt and empower vice. Our corrupt taxation system must be reset.

Veteran's Assistance (VA)/Benefit Programs top our nation's most fraudulent and wasteful expenses. The VA program should support the truly disabled and families of fallen heroes alone. A "Working Patriots Program" should be implemented to aid veterans of DoD, Law Enforcement, Fire Fighters, etc. with return to civilian life. These programs and their recipients must be routinely audited for FWA.

Nationwide DoD, VA and Public Health Services are redundant and ineffective throughout our nation. Military healthcare programs should support operational medicine with Research and Development only. Civilian Healthcare services should support NDA and stateside DoD medical needs. All Federally funded hospitals, clinics and services should be reassessed for viability, and sold/transferred to civilian health services, with military health professionals assigned to such as augmented staffing, providing hands-on training to operational providers on state-of-art systems. Such an initiative would expand a Tri-Care style initiative to all American beneficiaries.

State Fiscal Responsibilities

The Constitution's 10th Amendment delegates individual State oversight to manage and establish financial responsibility of programs and actions not specifically delineated within our Constitution and Laws. As such, Federal actions for the following should be significantly constrained or cease all together, allowing the responsible State to entice enterprise and citizenry based on the success of their programs and offerings. Such competition will ensure politicians are held accountable while creating an even playing field and better environment for all. Here's a few programs that could be deferred to the States:

- Crime (yet maintaining Federal standards and oversight)
- Domestic Federal Aid (State Welfare and Non-Profit plans)
- Drug and Alcohol Oversight
- Educational Programs (All Levels)
- Energy Creation and Management (included in Commerce)
- Environment (with Federal Audit/Monitoring)
- Gambling Programs (Not a form of Commerce)
- Healthcare (Federal & DoD Employees receive stipends)
- Housing Standards
- Natural Resources
- Pornography and Sexual Deviancy (In tandem with FTC)
- Private Business
- Transportation

National Defense

U. S. C. Article 1, Section 8 gives Congress **Fiscal Oversight,** while Article 2, Section 2 assigns the President the **Operational Oversight**. The 2nd Amendment confirms that *We the People* must not have our *rights infringed*, ensuring our ability to *keep and bear Arms,* as a component *to ensure the security of* our *free State* and nation. A well-armed citizenry is our nation's greatest defense against enemies foreign and domestic. Those desiring to disarm the citizenry are bent on treason and tyranny.

Terrorism is the new warfront with enemies within and without our own borders. All National Defense assets must be adequately funded, armed, trained and supported for the protection of America's citizenry against all enemies, foreign and domestic, known and anticipated. *President Trump's* quick, precise and effective assassination of affirmed Terrorist foreign enemies is an example of proper Defense.

Border Invasion is an act of terrorism and must be fought in a similar manner as any war. Our Immigration laws must comply with the *U. S. Constitution* and must be fully implemented and observed. Violators must be identified, examined and managed according to laws with those who violate the laws being captured and prosecuted as a terrorist. Homeland Security, I. C. E. and State Law enforcement must work in concert with one another and with the U. S. Military as necessary. *"The*

United States shall guarantee to every State in this Union a Republican Form of Government and shall protect each of them against Invasion;". (U. S. C. Article 4, Section 4).

<u>Infrastructure, Information System Security and Energy Programs</u> are the 2nd most significant border for our National Defense. Strong oversight at Federal, State and Militia levels for each of these programs is essential for to the survival of our nation.

<u>Fraud, waste and abuse (FWA)</u> is rampant throughout the DoD, VA and every government program. The Strategic Defense Plan along with all Federal programs that support our national security must address and deter wasteful and unnecessary programs, repurposing funds to support new initiatives, and dissuade unessential enterprises. A well-balanced, adequately trained and lean militia is critical to our national defense.

Chapter 27 – Playing the TRUMP Card

America was founded by people who believed that God was their rock of safety. He is ours. I recognize we must be cautious in claiming that God is on our side, but I think it's all right to keep asking if we're on His side. Ronald Reagan, State of the Union Address, Jan. 25, 1984

I lift up my eyes to the mountains-- where does my help come from? My help comes from the LORD, the Maker of heaven and earth. Psalms 121:1-2, NIV

~~~~~

It's obvious that the *King of Wildcards* was played by *Providence* to reveal the hands of key players around the globe, including those of us watching from the sidelines - forcing all to anti-up or fold.

As Abraham Lincoln so eloquently prophesied:

> *"At what point then is the approach of danger to be expected? I answer. If it ever reach us it must spring up amongst us; it cannot come from abroad. If destruction be our lot, we must ourselves be its author and finisher. As a nation of freemen, we must live through all time or die by suicide."*

While our nation stumbles towards the gallows of her own making, I believe that repentant prayers were the reason for the reshuffle and dealing of the Trump Card. Yet, the players who've failed to take the Trump Card out of play over the last 4 years, are now playing their hidden Ace as they bet all against our nation. Here's the latest:

COVID-19, Market Manipulation & Biden Hoax

Corona (COVID-19) Crisis is play #1 – Create a panic (bluff) with a simple virus like the *Common Cold*, closing-down as many pleasures and business as possible. Here's a quick reflection, COVID vs H1N1 Flu:

2020 COVID-19 Virus (as of March 25th, 2020),
Global: Infected = 350,000, Deaths = 14,510
U. S.:   Infected =   33,404, Deaths = 1,031
(80% > 60 years old and nearly all unhealthy)

2009 H1N1 virus (April 2009-April 2010),
Global: Infected = 60,800,000, Deaths = up to 575,400
U. S.:   Hospitalized = 274,000, Deaths = 12,469
(80% < 65 years old and mostly healthy)

(PS: As of printing these numbers obviously have increased, but I wholeheartedly doubt any numbers for COVID since there is financial and political gain for falsifying data.)

Appendix II provides a CDC chart displaying the mortality rates by age for the top 25 causes of death. Very insightful data that further reveals the Corona Virus (COVID-19) panic wouldn't even make the chart. It also reveals that only 15.6% of Americans live past 65 anyway with .1% of these dying from Flu/Pneumonia.

The Stock Market Crisis is play #2 – Similar to the Manufactured Market Crash of the Roaring 20's, key players have capitalized on COVID-19 to instill panic around the globe by crashing our stock market and shutting down businesses and family gatherings.

Wealthy Hedge Fund Managers, Media Moguls, Politicians, and others are manipulating the Stock Exchange while vocally promoting fear and uncertainty from their positions of influence. As millionaires & billionaires continue to play the ups and downs of the market, and government employees solidify their Retirement Plans (FERS), businesses and the working class have their hard-earned investments and retirement programs shaken.

The below graph shows the billionaire counts within the top 10 nations. Could the 476 Billionaires in China effect our market? Sure could!!!

World Rank	Country or Dependency	Total # of $B-airs	Richest in the country or dependency	Richest net worth in billions USD (year)
1	United States	585	Jeff Bezos	113 (2019)
2	China	476	Ma Huateng	38.8 (2019)
3	India[4]	131	Mukesh Ambani	60.8 (2019)
4	Germany	114	Beate Heister and Karl Albrecht Jr.	31.1 (2017)
5	Russia	96	Leonid Mikhelson	18.4 (2017)
6	Hong Kong	67	Li Ka-shing	37.7 (2018)
7	United Kingdom	54	Hinduja family	19.8 (2018)
8	Brazil	43	Jorge Paulo Lemann	29.7 (2018)
9	Italy	42	Maria Franca Fissolo	28 (2018)
10	Canada	39	David Thomson	27.2 (2017)

Top-10 Nation's with the Greatest Number of $ Billionaires

The Media / Biden Effect is play #3 – Not that Biden is a player but is a simple IOU on the table, revealing the true strategy of Corona and the Market Crisis. The true intent is to divide the U.S. and her allies, retake the White House and usher in a destructive globalist plan.

As noted earlier, a similar play was used 100 years ago against Republican President Herbert Hoover during his booming economy of the *Roaring Twenties*. A successful businessman and humanitarian who brought the nation hope and prosperity after a painful 1st World War, was taken out after his first term by a sudden (and mysterious) drop in the U. S. and global Markets. The ensuing panic caused a global Market crash, the Great Depression and eventually our terrible World War II.

History books don't promote this theory, but I am certain that the American elite and wealthy wanted to regain the White House and control of America and the global market. Pulling their funds from the Stock Market ushered in Franklin Roosevelt and decades of Democratic control. It made the wealthy elite even wealthier and enslaved generations within Roosevelt's Welfare programs.

Such *Crisis* are right out of the Alinsky and Marx playbooks: Instill an elite power that would rule the masses, create a crisis, pit people against one another, and then destroy all who are unwilling to become slaves to the elite. *A designed Crisis for an Elite purpose!*

No.	Name	Net worth (USD)	Age	Nationality	Source(s) of wealth
1 —	Jeff Bezos	$131 billion ▲	55	United States	Amazon
2 —	Bill Gates	$96.5 billion ▲	63	United States	Microsoft
3 —	Warren Buffett	$82.5 billion ▼	88	United States	Berkshire Hathaway
4 —	Bernard Arnault	$76 billion ▲	70	France	LVMH
5 ▲	Carlos Slim	$64 billion ▼	79	Mexico	América Móvil, Grupo Carso
6 —	Amancio Ortega	$62.7 billion ▼	82	Spain	Inditex, Zara
7 ▲	Larry Ellison	$62.5 billion ▲	74	United States	Oracle Corporation
8 ▼	Mark Zuckerberg	$62.3 billion ▼	34	United States	Facebook
9 ▲	Michael Bloomberg	$55.5 billion ▲	77	United States	Bloomberg L.P.
10 ▲	Larry Page	$50.8 billion ▲	45	United States	Alphabet Inc.

Forbes 2019 Top 10 List of the World's Wealthiest

The Forbes 2019 list of the worlds' top 10 wealthiest shown above reveals 6 of the 7 wealthiest Americans as leaders in the charge against our *Trump Card*. During the last 4 plus years, along with their

Mainstream Media and Politically Elite, continuous attacks have been directed against our President, his administration and his proposed actions. As of this writing, the Russia Hoax (*Operation Crossfire Hurricane*) remains in headline news along with suggestions of impeachment over his COVID and Market responses, any other issue conjured-up by the Slave Party.

It's my opinion that *We the People* and *Mr. Trump* must act soon and courageously, playing the *Declaration and Constitution* cards in defense of the assault on our nation and the world. America's new energy independence and global strength is a building block for America to not only survive but prosper during this season of attack on the American and World economies. But **we must play boldly**.

Though the enemy is willing to lose all that we cherish, I believe that We the People still have a play. The **Dealer** could guide the table and the *Trump Card* in a way that none would expect, possibly winning both the present hand as well as our long-fought Civil War. The slaves will be freed, our children rescued and the future promising for our nation as well as the world. The Enemy comes to Steal, Kill and Destroy, but the *God of nature and nature's God* has given us this nation and time to reveal His plan. A plan confirming that *All men are created equal, and endowed with Life, Liberty and the ability to Pursue Happiness*!

Let us fall on our knees before the Creator of all things in thanksgiving and humility, pledging that *We the People* will stand and fight!

Two-hundred and forty-four years ago - *"our fathers brought forth on this continent, a new nation, conceived in Liberty, and dedicated to the proposition that all men are created equal. Now we are engaged in a great civil war, testing whether that nation, or any nation so conceived and so dedicated, can long endure… that this nation, under God, shall have a new birth of freedom -- and that government of the people, by the people, for the people, shall not perish from the earth."*

Abraham Lincoln - November 19, 1863 / Dan Wilson (edit) – March 30, 2020

Subsequent note:

My hope and prayer are that scriptural prophesies of *John's Revelation* remain in the distant future, but it's hard not to believe we're nearing the foretold apocalyptic end as this *"beloved"* disciple of Jesus reveals:

> *"It (the Beast) also forced all people, great and small, rich and poor, free and slave, to receive a mark on their right hands or on their foreheads, so that they could not buy or sell unless they had the mark, which is the name of the beast or the number of its name."* Rev 13:16-17, NIV

Those that relate the rich to the *"Mark of the Beast"*, I certainly understand your hesitance to seek happiness and/or wealth. You may even desire to leave it all behind and get off the grid. Yet I'd caution you about hiding your talent and never playing in the game of life. Those who don't play the game can never win, while the brave jump-in, learn the rules, and then play to overcome. *"For you did not receive the spirit of bondage again to fear, but you received the Spirit of adoption by whom we cry out, 'Abba, Father'."* Rom 8:15 NKJV

King Solomon is said to be the wealthiest man ever, receiving 666 "kikar" (1 King 10:14) of gold annually. Although Jeff Bezos is the supposed wealthiest man alive, I believe Bill Gates has more wealth when you include his Foundation into their assets. Though I question the *Beast* as being a man, the concept of *buying and selling* as outlined in *John's Revelations* certainly seems possible considering the reality of electronic currency (bitcoin, etc.).

With Gates being a leading player in the *Global Virus Pandemic* concern and promoting inoculations and tracking of every human through a chip or other, it's certainly seems conceivable that such a program could lead to a *Mark*. As I understand it, the push is to require all humans (poorest to wealthiest) to be inoculated and tracked by a computer chip placed on their body.

As things unfold through 2020, let's pray that we (and those we love) are given wisdom and shown grace to avoid any trap set by the enemy of our souls. But this is the discussion for a potential book to come your way soon.

"... the love of money is a root of all kinds of evil." (1 Tim 6:10, NIV).

May God bless us His creation, as we hold our standards and expectations high while we strive to serve one another!

May God bless the words and thoughts of this book.

May God honor those of integrity and graciousness.

May God bless the United States of America.

May God bless our cousins around the globe.

May God bless all who seek Life, Liberty and Happiness.

Note: Reference to individuals and/or organizations within this book does not constitute or suggest any formal or informal agreements, endorsements or appointments by the individual/organization, their sponsors, management or employees for either the author or opinions expressed.

Declaration of Independence

The Unanimous Declaration of the Thirteen United States of America

When in the Course of human events, it becomes necessary for one people to dissolve the political bands which have connected them with another, and to assume among the powers of the earth, the separate and equal station to which the Laws of Nature and of Nature's God entitle them, a decent respect to the opinions of mankind requires that they should declare the causes which impel them to the separation.

We hold these truths to be self-evident, that all men are created equal, that they are endowed by their Creator with certain unalienable Rights, that among these are Life, Liberty and the pursuit of Happiness.--That to secure these rights, Governments are instituted among Men, deriving their just powers from the consent of the governed, -- That whenever any Form of Government becomes destructive of these ends, it is the Right of the People to alter or to abolish it, and to institute new Government, laying its foundation on such principles and organizing its powers in such form, as to them shall seem most likely to effect their Safety and Happiness. Prudence, indeed, will dictate that Governments long established should not be changed for light and transient causes; and accordingly all experience hath shewn, that mankind are more disposed to suffer, while evils are sufferable, than to right themselves by abolishing the forms to which they are accustomed. But when a long train of abuses and usurpations, pursuing invariably the same Object evinces a design to reduce them under absolute Despotism, it is their right, it is their duty, to throw off such Government, and to provide new Guards for their future security.--Such has been the patient sufferance of these Colonies; and such is now the necessity which constrains them to alter their former Systems of Government. The history of the present King of Great Britain is a history of repeated injuries and usurpations, all having in direct object the establishment of an absolute Tyranny over these States. To prove this, let Facts be submitted to a candid world.

He has refused his Assent to Laws, the most wholesome and necessary for the public good.

He has forbidden his Governors to pass Laws of immediate and pressing importance, unless suspended in their operation till his Assent should be obtained; and when so suspended, he has utterly neglected to attend to them.

He has refused to pass other Laws for the accommodation of large districts of people, unless those people would relinquish the right of Representation in the Legislature, a right inestimable to them and formidable to tyrants only.

He has called together legislative bodies at places unusual, uncomfortable, and distant from the depository of their public Records, for the sole purpose of fatiguing them into compliance with his measures.

He has dissolved Representative Houses repeatedly, for opposing with manly firmness his invasions on the rights of the people.

He has refused for a long time, after such dissolutions, to cause others to be elected; whereby the Legislative powers, incapable of Annihilation, have returned to the People at large for their exercise; the State remaining in the meantime exposed to all the dangers of invasion from without, and convulsions within.

He has endeavoured to prevent the population of these States; for that purpose obstructing the Laws for Naturalization of Foreigners; refusing to pass others to encourage their migrations hither, and raising the conditions of new Appropriations of Lands.

He has obstructed the Administration of Justice, by refusing his Assent to Laws for establishing Judiciary powers.

He has made Judges dependent on his Will alone, for the tenure of their offices, and the amount and payment of their salaries.

He has erected a multitude of New Offices, and sent hither swarms of Officers to harrass our people, and eat out their substance.

He has kept among us, in times of peace, Standing Armies without the Consent of our legislatures.

He has affected to render the Military independent of and superior to the Civil power.

He has combined with others to subject us to a jurisdiction foreign to our constitution, and unacknowledged by our laws; giving his Assent to their Acts of pretended Legislation:

For Quartering large bodies of armed troops among us:

For protecting them, by a mock Trial, from punishment for any Murders which they should commit on the Inhabitants of these States:

>*For cutting off our Trade with all parts of the world:*

>*For imposing Taxes on us without our Consent:*

>*For depriving us in many cases, of the benefits of Trial by Jury:*

>*For transporting us beyond Seas to be tried for pretended offences*

>*For abolishing the free System of English Laws in a neighbouring Province, establishing therein an Arbitrary government, and enlarging its Boundaries so as to render it at once an example and fit instrument for introducing the same absolute rule into these Colonies:*

>*For taking away our Charters, abolishing our most valuable Laws, and altering fundamentally the Forms of our Governments:*

>*For suspending our own Legislatures, and declaring themselves invested with power to legislate for us in all cases whatsoever.*

He has abdicated Government here, by declaring us out of his Protection and waging War against us.

He has plundered our seas, ravaged our Coasts, burnt our towns, and destroyed the lives of our people.

He is at this time transporting large Armies of foreign Mercenaries to compleat the works of death, desolation and tyranny, already begun with circumstances of Cruelty & perfidy scarcely paralleled in the most barbarous ages, and totally unworthy the Head of a civilized nation.

He has constrained our fellow Citizens taken Captive on the high Seas to bear Arms against their Country, to become the executioners of their friends and Brethren, or to fall themselves by their Hands.

He has excited domestic insurrections amongst us, and has endeavoured to bring on the inhabitants of our frontiers, the merciless Indian Savages, whose known rule of warfare, is an undistinguished destruction of all ages, sexes and conditions.

In every stage of these Oppressions We have Petitioned for Redress in the most humble terms: Our repeated Petitions have been answered only by repeated injury. A Prince whose character is thus marked by every act which may define a Tyrant, is unfit to be the ruler of a free people.

Nor have We been wanting in attentions to our Brittish brethren. We have warned them from time to time of attempts by their legislature to extend an unwarrantable jurisdiction over us. We have reminded them of the circumstances of our emigration and settlement here. We have appealed to their native justice and magnanimity, and we have conjured them by the ties of our common kindred to disavow these usurpations, which, would inevitably interrupt our connections and correspondence. They too have been deaf to the voice of justice and of consanguinity. We must, therefore, acquiesce in the necessity, which denounces our Separation, and hold them, as we hold the rest of mankind, Enemies in War, in Peace Friends.

We, therefore, the Representatives of the united States of America, in General Congress, Assembled, appealing to the Supreme Judge of the world for the rectitude of our intentions, do, in the Name, and by Authority of the good People of these Colonies, solemnly publish and declare, That these United Colonies are, and of Right ought to be Free and Independent States; that they are Absolved from all Allegiance to the British Crown, and that all political connection between them and the State of Great Britain, is and ought to be totally dissolved; and that as Free and Independent States, they have full Power to levy War, conclude Peace, contract Alliances, establish Commerce, and to do all other Acts and Things which Independent States may of right do. And for the support of this Declaration, with a firm reliance on the protection of divine Providence, we mutually pledge to each other our Lives, our Fortunes and our sacred Honor. shall consist of a Senate and House of Representatives.

United States Constitution

Preamble

We the People of the United States, in Order to form a more perfect Union, establish Justice, insure domestic Tranquility, provide for the common defence, promote the general Welfare, and secure the Blessings of Liberty to ourselves and our Posterity, do ordain and establish this Constitution for the United States of America.

Article I - Legislative

Section 1

All legislative Powers herein granted shall be vested in a Congress of the United States, which shall consist of a Senate and House of Representatives.

Section 2

1: The House of Representatives shall be composed of Members chosen every second Year by the People of the several States, and the Electors in each State shall have the Qualifications requisite for Electors of the most numerous Branch of the State Legislature.

2: No Person shall be a Representative who shall not have attained to the Age of twenty five Years, and been seven Years a Citizen of the United States, and who shall not, when elected, be an Inhabitant of that State in which he shall be chosen.

3: Representatives and direct Taxes shall be apportioned among the several States which may be included within this Union, according to their respective Numbers, which shall be determined by adding to the whole Number of free Persons, including those bound to Service for a Term of Years, and excluding Indians not taxed, three fifths of all other Persons.2 The actual Enumeration shall be made within three Years after the first Meeting of the Congress of the United States, and within every subsequent Term of ten Years, in such Manner as they shall by Law direct. The Number of Representatives shall not exceed one for every thirty Thousand, but each State shall have at Least one Representative; and until such enumeration shall be made, the State of New Hampshire shall be entitled to chuse three, Massachusetts eight, Rhode-Island and Providence Plantations one, Connecticut five, New-York six, New Jersey four, Pennsylvania eight, Delaware one, Maryland six, Virginia ten, North Carolina five, South Carolina five, and Georgia three.

4: When vacancies happen in the Representation from any State, the Executive Authority thereof shall issue Writs of Election to fill such Vacancies.

5: The House of Representatives shall chuse their Speaker and other Officers; and shall have the sole Power of Impeachment.

Section 3

1: The Senate of the United States shall be composed of two Senators from each State, chosen by the Legislature thereof,3 for six Years; and each Senator shall have one Vote.

2: Immediately after they shall be assembled in Consequence of the first Election, they shall be divided as equally as may be into three Classes. The Seats of the Senators of the first Class shall be vacated at the Expiration of the second Year, of the second Class at the Expiration of the fourth Year, and of the third Class at the Expiration of the sixth Year, so that one third may be chosen every second Year; and if Vacancies happen by Resignation, or otherwise, during the Recess of the Legislature of any State, the Executive thereof may make temporary Appointments until the next Meeting of the Legislature, which shall then fill such Vacancies.4

3: No Person shall be a Senator who shall not have attained to the Age of thirty Years, and been nine Years a Citizen of the United States, and who shall not, when elected, be an Inhabitant of that State for which he shall be chosen.

4: The Vice President of the United States shall be President of the Senate, but shall have no Vote, unless they be equally divided.

5: The Senate shall chuse their other Officers, and also a President pro tempore, in the Absence of the Vice President, or when he shall exercise the Office of President of the United States.

6: The Senate shall have the sole Power to try all Impeachments. When sitting for that Purpose, they shall be on Oath or Affirmation. When the President of the United States is tried, the Chief Justice shall preside: And no Person shall be convicted without the Concurrence of two thirds of the Members present.

7: Judgment in Cases of impeachment shall not extend further than to removal from Office, and disqualification to hold and enjoy any Office of honor, Trust or Profit under the United States: but the Party convicted shall nevertheless be liable and subject to Indictment, Trial, Judgment and Punishment, according to Law.

Section 4

1: The Times, Places and Manner of holding Elections for Senators and Representatives, shall be prescribed in each State by the Legislature thereof; but the Congress may at any time by Law make or alter such Regulations, except as to the Places of chusing Senators.

2: The Congress shall assemble at least once in every Year, and such Meeting shall be on the first Monday in December,5 unless they shall by Law appoint a different Day.

Section 5

1: Each House shall be the Judge of the Elections, Returns and Qualifications of its own Members, and a Majority of each shall constitute a Quorum to do Business; but a smaller Number may adjourn from day to day, and may be authorized to compel the Attendance of absent Members, in such Manner, and under such Penalties as each House may provide.

2: Each House may determine the Rules of its Proceedings, punish its Members for disorderly Behaviour, and, with the Concurrence of two thirds, expel a Member.

3: Each House shall keep a Journal of its Proceedings, and from time to time publish the same, excepting such Parts as may in their Judgment require Secrecy; and the Yeas and Nays of the Members of either House on any question shall, at the Desire of one fifth of those Present, be entered on the Journal.

4: Neither House, during the Session of Congress, shall, without the Consent of the other, adjourn for more than three days, nor to any other Place than that in which the two Houses shall be sitting.

Section 6

1: The Senators and Representatives shall receive a Compensation for their Services, to be ascertained by Law, and paid out of the Treasury of the United States.6 They shall in all Cases, except Treason, Felony and Breach of the Peace, be privileged from Arrest during their Attendance at the Session of their respective Houses, and in going to and returning from the same; and for any Speech or Debate in either House, they shall not be questioned in any other Place.

2: No Senator or Representative shall, during the Time for which he was elected, be appointed to any civil Office under the Authority of the United States, which shall have been created, or the Emoluments whereof shall have been encreased during such time; and no Person holding any Office under the United States, shall be a Member of either House during his Continuance in Office.

Section 7

1: All Bills for raising Revenue shall originate in the House of Representatives; but the Senate may propose or concur with Amendments as on other Bills.

2: Every Bill which shall have passed the House of Representatives and the Senate, shall, before it become a Law, be presented to the President of the United States; If he approve he shall sign it, but if not he shall return it, with his Objections to that House in which it shall have originated, who shall enter the Objections at large on their Journal, and proceed to reconsider it. If after such Reconsideration two thirds of that House shall agree to pass the Bill, it shall be sent, together with the Objections, to the other House, by which it shall likewise be reconsidered, and if approved by two thirds of that House, it shall become a Law. But in all such Cases the Votes of both Houses shall be determined by yeas and Nays, and the Names of the Persons voting for and against the Bill shall be entered on the Journal of each House respectively. If any Bill shall not be returned by the President within ten Days (Sundays excepted) after it shall have been presented to him, the Same shall be a Law, in like Manner as if he had signed it, unless the Congress by their Adjournment prevent its Return, in which Case it shall not be a Law.

3: Every Order, Resolution, or Vote to which the Concurrence of the Senate and House of Representatives may be necessary (except on a question of Adjournment) shall be presented to the President of the United States; and before the Same shall take Effect, shall be approved by him, or being disapproved by him, shall be repassed by two thirds of the Senate and House of Representatives, according to the Rules and Limitations prescribed in the Case of a Bill.

Section 8

1: The Congress shall have Power To lay and collect Taxes, Duties, Imposts and Excises, to pay the Debts and provide for the common Defence and general Welfare of the United States; but all Duties, Imposts and Excises shall be uniform throughout the United States;

2: To borrow Money on the credit of the United States;

3: To regulate Commerce with foreign Nations, and among the several States, and with the Indian Tribes;

4: To establish an uniform Rule of Naturalization, and uniform Laws on the subject of Bankruptcies throughout the United States;

5: To coin Money, regulate the Value thereof, and of foreign Coin, and fix the Standard of Weights and Measures;

6: To provide for the Punishment of counterfeiting the Securities and current Coin of the United States;

7: To establish Post Offices and post Roads;

8: To promote the Progress of Science and useful Arts, by securing for limited Times to Authors and Inventors the exclusive Right to their respective Writings and Discoveries;

9: To constitute Tribunals inferior to the supreme Court;

10: To define and punish Piracies and Felonies committed on the high Seas, and Offences against the Law of Nations;

11: To declare War, grant Letters of Marque and Reprisal, and make Rules concerning Captures on Land and Water;

12: To raise and support Armies, but no Appropriation of Money to that Use shall be for a longer Term than two Years;

13: To provide and maintain a Navy;

14: To make Rules for the Government and Regulation of the land and naval Forces;

15: To provide for calling forth the Militia to execute the Laws of the Union, suppress Insurrections and repel Invasions;

16: To provide for organizing, arming, and disciplining, the Militia, and for governing such Part of them as may be employed in the Service of the United States, reserving to the States respectively, the Appointment of the Officers, and the Authority of training the Militia according to the discipline prescribed by Congress;

17: To exercise exclusive Legislation in all Cases whatsoever, over such District (not exceeding ten Miles square) as may, by Cession of particular States, and the Acceptance of Congress, become the Seat of the Government of the United States, and to exercise like Authority over all Places purchased by the Consent of the Legislature of the State in which the Same shall be, for the Erection of Forts, Magazines, Arsenals, dock-Yards, and other needful Buildings;—And

18: To make all Laws which shall be necessary and proper for carrying into Execution the foregoing Powers, and all other Powers vested by this Constitution in the Government of the United States, or in any Department or Officer thereof.

Section 9

1: The Migration or Importation of such Persons as any of the States now existing shall think proper to admit, shall not be prohibited by the Congress prior to the Year one thousand eight hundred and eight, but a Tax or duty may be imposed on such Importation, not exceeding ten dollars for each Person.

2: The Privilege of the Writ of Habeas Corpus shall not be suspended, unless when in Cases of Rebellion or Invasion the public Safety may require it.

3: No Bill of Attainder or ex post facto Law shall be passed.

4: No Capitation, or other direct, Tax shall be laid, unless in Proportion to the Census or Enumeration herein before directed to be taken.7

5: No Tax or Duty shall be laid on Articles exported from any State.

6: No Preference shall be given by any Regulation of Commerce or Revenue to the Ports of one State over those of another: nor shall Vessels bound to, or from, one State, be obliged to enter, clear, or pay Duties in another.

7: No Money shall be drawn from the Treasury, but in Consequence of Appropriations made by Law; and a regular Statement and Account of the Receipts and Expenditures of all public Money shall be published from time to time.

8: No Title of Nobility shall be granted by the United States: And no Person holding any Office of Profit or Trust under them, shall, without the Consent of the Congress, accept of any present, Emolument, Office, or Title, of any kind whatever, from any King, Prince, or foreign State.

Section 10

1: No State shall enter into any Treaty, Alliance, or Confederation; grant Letters of Marque and Reprisal; coin Money; emit Bills of Credit; make any Thing but gold and silver Coin a Tender in Payment of Debts; pass any Bill of Attainder, ex post facto Law, or Law impairing the Obligation of Contracts, or grant any Title of Nobility.

2: No State shall, without the Consent of the Congress, lay any Imposts or Duties on Imports or Exports, except what may be absolutely necessary for executing it's inspection Laws: and the net Produce of all Duties and Imposts, laid by any State on Imports or Exports, shall be for the Use of the Treasury of the United States; and all such Laws shall be subject to the Revision and Controul of the Congress.

3: No State shall, without the Consent of Congress, lay any Duty of Tonnage, keep Troops, or Ships of War in time of Peace, enter into any Agreement or Compact with another State, or with a foreign Power, or engage in War, unless actually invaded, or in such imminent Danger as will not admit of delay.

Article II - Executive

Section 1

1: The executive Power shall be vested in a President of the United States of America. He shall hold his Office during the Term of four Years, and, together with the Vice President, chosen for the same Term, be elected, as follows

2: Each State shall appoint, in such Manner as the Legislature thereof may direct, a Number of Electors, equal to the whole Number of Senators and Representatives to which the State may be entitled in the Congress: but no Senator or Representative, or Person holding an Office of Trust or Profit under the United States, shall be appointed an Elector.

3: The Electors shall meet in their respective States, and vote by Ballot for two Persons, of whom one at least shall not be an Inhabitant of the same State with themselves. And they shall make a List of all the Persons voted for, and of the Number of Votes for each; which List they shall sign and certify, and transmit sealed to the Seat of the Government of the United States, directed to the President of the Senate. The President of the Senate shall, in the Presence of the Senate and House of Representatives, open all the Certificates, and the Votes shall then be counted. The Person having the greatest Number of Votes shall be the President, if such Number be a Majority of the whole Number of Electors appointed; and if there be more than one who have such Majority, and have an equal Number of Votes, then the House of Representatives shall immediately chuse by Ballot one of them for President; and if no Person have a Majority, then from the five highest on the List the said House shall in like Manner chuse the President. But in chusing the President, the Votes shall be taken by States, the Representation from each State having one Vote; A quorum for this Purpose shall consist of a Member or Members from two thirds of the States, and a Majority of all the States shall be necessary to a Choice. In every Case, after the Choice of the President, the Person having the greatest Number of Votes of the Electors shall be the Vice President. But if there should remain two or more who have equal Votes, the Senate shall chuse from them by Ballot the Vice President.8

4: The Congress may determine the Time of chusing the Electors, and the Day on which they shall give their Votes; which Day shall be the same throughout the United States.

5: No Person except a natural born Citizen, or a Citizen of the United States, at the time of the Adoption of this Constitution, shall be eligible to the Office of President; neither shall any Person be eligible to that Office who shall not have attained to the Age of thirty five Years, and been fourteen Years a Resident within the United States.

6: In Case of the Removal of the President from Office, or of his Death, Resignation, or Inability to discharge the Powers and Duties of the said Office,9 the Same shall devolve on the Vice President, and the Congress may by Law provide for the Case of Removal, Death, Resignation or Inability, both of the President and Vice President, declaring what Officer shall then act as President, and such Officer shall act accordingly, until the Disability be removed, or a President shall be elected.

7: The President shall, at stated Times, receive for his Services, a Compensation, which shall neither be encreased nor diminished during the Period for which he shall have been elected, and he shall not receive within that Period any other Emolument from the United States, or any of them.

8: Before he enter on the Execution of his Office, he shall take the following Oath or Affirmation:—"I do solemnly swear (or affirm) that I will faithfully execute the Office of President of the United States, and will to the best of my Ability, preserve, protect and defend the Constitution of the United States."

Section 2

1: The President shall be Commander in Chief of the Army and Navy of the United States, and of the Militia of the several States, when called into the actual Service of the United States; he may require the Opinion, in writing, of the principal Officer in each of the executive Departments, upon any Subject relating to the Duties of their respective Offices, and he shall have Power to grant Reprieves and Pardons for Offences against the United States, except in Cases of Impeachment.

2: He shall have Power, by and with the Advice and Consent of the Senate, to make Treaties, provided two thirds of the Senators present concur; and he shall nominate, and by and with the Advice and Consent of the Senate, shall appoint Ambassadors, other public Ministers and Consuls, Judges of the supreme Court, and all other Officers of the United States, whose Appointments are not herein otherwise provided for, and which shall be established by Law: but the Congress may by Law vest the Appointment of such inferior Officers, as they think proper, in the President alone, in the Courts of Law, or in the Heads of Departments.

3: The President shall have Power to fill up all Vacancies that may happen during the Recess of the Senate, by granting Commissions which shall expire at the End of their next Session.

Section 3

He shall from time to time give to the Congress Information of the State of the Union, and recommend to their Consideration such Measures as he shall judge necessary and expedient; he may, on extraordinary Occasions, convene both Houses, or either of them, and in Case of Disagreement between them, with Respect to the Time of Adjournment, he may adjourn them to such Time as he shall think proper; he shall receive Ambassadors and other public Ministers; he shall take Care that the Laws be faithfully executed, and shall Commission all the Officers of the United States.

Section 4

The President, Vice President and all civil Officers of the United States, shall be removed from Office on Impeachment for, and Conviction of, Treason, Bribery, or other high Crimes and Misdemeanors.

Article III - Judicial

Section 1

The judicial Power of the United States, shall be vested in one supreme Court, and in such inferior Courts as the Congress may from time to time ordain and establish. The Judges, both of the supreme and inferior Courts, shall hold their Offices during good

Behaviour, and shall, at stated Times, receive for their Services, a Compensation, which shall not be diminished during their Continuance in Office.

<u>Section 2</u>

1: The judicial Power shall extend to all Cases, in Law and Equity, arising under this Constitution, the Laws of the United States, and Treaties made, or which shall be made, under their Authority;—to all Cases affecting Ambassadors, other public Ministers and Consuls;—to all Cases of admiralty and maritime Jurisdiction;—to Controversies to which the United States shall be a Party;—to Controversies between two or more States;—between a State and Citizens of another State;10 —between Citizens of different States, —between Citizens of the same State claiming Lands under Grants of different States, and between a State, or the Citizens thereof, and foreign States, Citizens or Subjects.

2: In all Cases affecting Ambassadors, other public Ministers and Consuls, and those in which a State shall be Party, the supreme Court shall have original Jurisdiction. In all the other Cases before mentioned, the supreme Court shall have appellate Jurisdiction, both as to Law and Fact, with such Exceptions, and under such Regulations as the Congress shall make.

3: The Trial of all Crimes, except in Cases of Impeachment, shall be by Jury; and such Trial shall be held in the State where the said Crimes shall have been committed; but when not committed within any State, the Trial shall be at such Place or Places as the Congress may by Law have directed.

<u>Section 3</u>

1: Treason against the United States, shall consist only in levying War against them, or in adhering to their Enemies, giving them Aid and Comfort. No Person shall be convicted of Treason unless on the Testimony of two Witnesses to the same overt Act, or on Confession in open Court.

2: The Congress shall have Power to declare the Punishment of Treason, but no Attainder of Treason shall work Corruption of Blood, or Forfeiture except during the Life of the Person attainted.

Article IV - States' Relations

<u>Section 1</u>

Full Faith and Credit shall be given in each State to the public Acts, Records, and judicial Proceedings of every other State. And the Congress may by general Laws prescribe the Manner in which such Acts, Records and Proceedings shall be proved, and the Effect thereof.

<u>Section 2</u>

1: The Citizens of each State shall be entitled to all Privileges and Immunities of Citizens in the several States.

2: A Person charged in any State with Treason, Felony, or other Crime, who shall flee from Justice, and be found in another State, shall on Demand of the executive Authority of the State from which he fled, be delivered up, to be removed to the State having Jurisdiction of the Crime.

3: No Person held to Service or Labour in one State, under the Laws thereof, escaping into another, shall, in Consequence of any Law or Regulation therein, be discharged from such Service or Labour, but shall be delivered up on Claim of the Party to whom such Service or Labour may be due.11

Section 3

1: New States may be admitted by the Congress into this Union; but no new State shall be formed or erected within the Jurisdiction of any other State; nor any State be formed by the Junction of two or more States, or Parts of States, without the Consent of the Legislatures of the States concerned as well as of the Congress.

2: The Congress shall have Power to dispose of and make all needful Rules and Regulations respecting the Territory or other Property belonging to the United States; and nothing in this Constitution shall be so construed as to Prejudice any Claims of the United States, or of any particular State.

Section 4

The United States shall guarantee to every State in this Union a Republican Form of Government, and shall protect each of them against Invasion; and on Application of the Legislature, or of the Executive (when the Legislature cannot be convened) against domestic Violence.

Article V - Mode of Amendment

The Congress, whenever two thirds of both Houses shall deem it necessary, shall propose Amendments to this Constitution, or, on the Application of the Legislatures of two thirds of the several States, shall call a Convention for proposing Amendments, which, in either Case, shall be valid to all Intents and Purposes, as Part of this Constitution, when ratified by the Legislatures of three fourths of the several States, or by Conventions in three fourths thereof, as the one or the other Mode of Ratification may be proposed by the Congress; Provided that no Amendment which may be made prior to the Year One thousand eight hundred and eight shall in any Manner affect the first and fourth Clauses in the Ninth Section of the first Article; and that no State, without its Consent, shall be deprived of its equal Suffrage in the Senate.

Article VI - Prior Debts, National Supremacy, Oaths of Office

1: All Debts contracted and Engagements entered into, before the Adoption of this Constitution, shall be as valid against the United States under this Constitution, as under the Confederation.

2: This Constitution, and the Laws of the United States which shall be made in Pursuance thereof; and all Treaties made, or which shall be made, under the Authority of the United States, shall be the supreme Law of the Land; and the Judges in every State shall be bound thereby, any Thing in the Constitution or Laws of any State to the Contrary notwithstanding.

3: The Senators and Representatives before mentioned, and the Members of the several State Legislatures, and all executive and judicial Officers, both of the United States and of the several States, shall be bound by Oath or Affirmation, to support this Constitution; but no religious Test shall ever be required as a Qualification to any Office or public Trust under the United States.

Article VII - Ratification

The Ratification of the Conventions of nine States, shall be sufficient for the Establishment of this Constitution between the States so ratifying the Same.

The Word "the", being interlined between the seventh and eight Lines of the first Page, The Word "Thirty" being partly written on an Erazure in the fifteenth Line of the first Page. The Words "is tried" being interlined between the thirty second and thirty third Lines of the first Page and the Word "the" being interlined between the forty third and forty fourth Lines of the second Page.

———

Done in Convention by the Unanimous Consent of the States present the Seventeenth Day of September in the Year of our Lord one thousand seven hundred and Eighty seven and of the Independence of the United States of America the Twelfth In witness whereof We have hereunto subscribed our Names,

Attest William Jackson Secretary

Go: Washington -Presidt. and deputy from Virginia

Delaware: Geo: Read, Gunning Bedford jun, John Dickinson, Richard Bassett, Jacob Broom
Maryland: James McHenry, Dan of St Thos. Jenifer, Danl Carroll
Virginia: John Blair, James Madison Jr.
North Carolina: Wm Blount, Richd. Dobbs Spaight, Hu Williamson
South Carolina; J. Rutledge, Charles Cotesworth Pinckney, Charles Pinckney, Pierce Butler
Georgia: William Few, Abr Baldwin
New Hampshire: John Langdon, Nicholas Gilman
Massachusetts; Nathaniel Gorham, Rufus King
Connecticut; Wm. Saml. Johnson, Roger Sherman
New York; Alexander Hamilton
New Jersey; Wil. Livingston, David Brearley, Wm. Paterson. Jona: Dayton
Pennsylvania; B Franklin, Thomas Mifflin, Robt Morris, Geo. Clymer, Thos. FitzSimons, Jared Ingersoll, James Wilson. Gouv Morris

Letter of Transmittal
In Convention. Monday September 17ᵗʰ, 1787

Present; The States of New Hampshire, Massachusetts, Connecticut, Mr. Hamilton from New York, New Jersey, Pennsylvania, Delaware, Maryland, Virginia, North Carolina, South Carolina and Georgia.

Resolved, That the preceeding Constitution be laid before the United States in Congress assembled, and that it is the Opinion of this Convention, that it should afterwards be submitted to a Convention of Delegates, chosen in each State by the People thereof, under the Recommendation of its Legislature, for their Assent and Ratification; and that each Convention assenting to, and ratifying the Same, should give Notice thereof to the United States in Congress assembled. Resolved, That it is the Opinion of this Convention, that as soon as the Conventions of nine States shall have ratified this Constitution, the United States in Congress assembled should fix a Day on which Electors should be appointed by the States which shall have ratified the same, and a Day on which the Electors should assemble to vote for the President, and the Time and Place for commencing Proceedings under this Constitution.

That after such Publication the Electors should be appointed, and the Senators and Representatives elected: That the Electors should meet on the Day fixed for the Election of the President, and should transmit their Votes certified, signed, sealed and directed, as the Constitution requires, to the Secretary of the United States in Congress assembled, that the Senators and Representatives should convene at the Time and Place assigned; that the Senators should appoint a President of the Senate, for the sole Purpose of receiving, opening and counting the Votes for President; and, that after he shall be chosen, the Congress, together with the President, should, without Delay, proceed to execute this Constitution.

By the unanimous Order of the Convention

W. Jackson Secretary.

Go: Washington -Presidt.

SIR:

We have now the honor to submit to the consideration of the United States in Congress assembled, that Constitution which has appeared to us the most advisable.

The friends of our country have long seen and desired that the power of making war, peace, and treaties, that of levying money, and regulating commerce, and the correspondent executive and judicial authorities, should be fully and effectually vested in the General Government of the Union; but the impropriety of delegating such extensive trust to one body of men is evident: hence results the necessity of a different organization.

It is obviously impracticable in the Federal Government of these States to secure all rights of independent sovereignty to each, and yet provide for the interest and safety of all. Individuals entering into society must give up a share of liberty to preserve the rest. The magnitude of the sacrifice must depend as well on situation and circumstance, as on the object to be obtained. It is at all times difficult to draw with precision the line between those rights which must be surrendered, and those which may be preserved; and, on the present occasion, this difficulty was increased by a difference among the several States as to their situation, extent, habits, and particular interests.

In all our deliberations on this subject, we kept steadily in our view that which appears to us the greatest interest of every true American, the consolidation of our Union, in which is involved our prosperity, felicity, safety—perhaps our national existence. This important consideration, seriously and deeply impressed on our minds, led each State in the Convention to be less rigid on points of inferior magnitude than might have been otherwise expected; and thus, the Constitution which we now present is the result of a spirit of amity, and of that mutual deference and concession, which the peculiarity of our political situation rendered indispensable.

That it will meet the full and entire approbation of every State is not, perhaps, to be expected; but each will, doubtless, consider, that had her interest alone been consulted, the consequences might have been particularly disagreeable or injurious to others; that it is liable to as few exceptions as could reasonably have been expected, we hope and believe; that it may promote the lasting welfare of that Country so dear to us all, and secure her freedom and happiness, is our most ardent wish.

With great respect, we have the honor to be,

SIR, your excellency's most obedient and humble servants:

GEORGE WASHINGTON, President.

By the unanimous order of the convention.

His Excellency, the President of Congress.

Bill of Rights - Preamble

Preamble

Congress OF THE United States, begun and held at the City of New-York, on Wednesday the fourth of March, one thousand seven hundred and eighty nine.

THE Conventions of a number of the States, having at the time of their adopting the Constitution, expressed a desire, in order to prevent misconstruction or abuse of its powers, that further declaratory and restrictive clauses should be added: And as extending the ground of public confidence in the Government, will best ensure the beneficent ends of its institution.

RESOLVED by the Senate and House of Representatives of the United States of America, in Congress assembled, two thirds of both Houses concurring, that the following Articles be proposed to the Legislatures of the several States, as amendments to the Constitution of the United States, all, or any of which Articles, when ratified by three fourths of the said Legislatures, to be valid to all intents and purposes, as part of the said Constitution; viz.

ARTICLES in addition to, and Amendment of the Constitution of the United States of America, proposed by Congress, and ratified by the Legislatures of the several States, pursuant to the fifth Article of the original Constitution.

Frederick Augustus Muhlenberg. Speaker of the House of Representatives

John Adams, Vice President of the United States and President of the Senate.

Attest,

John Beckley, Clerk of the House of Representatives.

Sam. A. Otis, Secretary of the Senate.

Article the first. .... After the first enumeration required by the first Article of the Constitution, there shall be one Representative for every thirty thousand, until the number shall amount to one hundred, after which, the proportion shall be so regulated by Congress, that there shall be not less than one hundred Representatives, nor less than one Representative for every forty thousand persons, until the number of Representatives shall amount to two hundred, after which the proportion shall be so regulated by Congress, that there shall not be less than two hundred Representatives, nor more than one Representative for every fifty thousand persons.

Article the second. .... No law, varying the compensation for the services of the Senators and Representatives, shall take effect, until an election of Representatives shall have intervened. see Amendment XXVII

Bill of Rights / Constitutional Amendments

Amendment 1 - Freedom of expression and religion (Article I)

Congress shall make no law respecting an establishment of religion, or prohibiting the free exercise thereof; or abridging the freedom of speech, or of the press; or the right of the people peaceably to assemble, and to petition the Government for a redress of grievances.

Amendment 2 - Bearing Arms (Article II)

A well regulated Militia, being necessary to the security of a free State, the right of the people to keep and bear Arms, shall not be infringed.

Amendment 3 - Quartering Soldiers (Article III)

No Soldier shall, in time of peace be quartered in any house, without the consent of the Owner, nor in time of war, but in a manner to be prescribed by law.

Amendment 4 - Search and Seizure (Article IV)

The right of the people to be secure in their persons, houses, papers, and effects, against unreasonable searches and seizures, shall not be violated, and no Warrants shall issue, but upon probable cause, supported by Oath or affirmation, and particularly describing the place to be searched, and the persons or things to be seized.

Amendment 5 - Rights of Persons (Article V)

No person shall be held to answer for a capital, or otherwise infamous crime, unless on a presentment or indictment of a Grand Jury, except in cases arising in the land or naval forces, or in the Militia, when in actual service in time of War or public danger; nor shall any person be subject for the same offence to be twice put in jeopardy of life or limb; nor shall be compelled in any criminal case to be a witness against himself, nor be deprived of life, liberty, or property, without due process of law; nor shall private property be taken for public use, without just compensation.

Amendment 6 - Rights of Accused in Criminal Prosecutions (Article VI)

In all criminal prosecutions, the accused shall enjoy the right to a speedy and public trial, by an impartial jury of the State and district wherein the crime shall have been committed, which district shall have been previously ascertained by law, and to be informed of the nature and cause of the accusation; to be confronted with the witnesses against him; to have compulsory process for obtaining witnesses in his favor, and to have the Assistance of Counsel for his defence.

Amendment 7 - Civil Trials (Article VII)

In Suits at common law, where the value in controversy shall exceed twenty dollars, the right of trial by jury shall be preserved, and no fact tried by a jury, shall be otherwise re-examined in any Court of the United States, than according to the rules of the common law.

Amendment 8 - Further Guarantees in Criminal Cases (Article VIII]

Excessive bail shall not be required, nor excessive fines imposed, nor cruel and unusual punishments inflicted.

Amendment 9 - Unenumerated Rights (Article IX]

The enumeration in the Constitution, of certain rights, shall not be construed to deny or disparage others retained by the people.

Amendment 10 - Reserved Powers (Article X]

The powers not delegated to the United States by the Constitution, nor prohibited by it to the States, are reserved to the States respectively, or to the people.

(End of the Bill of Rights)

Amendment 11 - Suits Against States

The Judicial power of the United States shall not be construed to extend to any suit in law or equity, commenced or prosecuted against one of the United States by Citizens of another State, or by Citizens or Subjects of any Foreign State.

Amendment 12 - Election of President

The Electors shall meet in their respective states, and vote by ballot for President and Vice-President, one of whom, at least, shall not be an inhabitant of the same state with themselves; they shall name in their ballots the person voted for as President, and in distinct ballots the person voted for as Vice-President, and they shall make distinct lists of all persons voted for as President, and of all persons voted for as Vice-President, and of the number of votes for each, which lists they shall sign and certify, and transmit sealed to the seat of the government of the United States, directed to the President of the Senate;—The President of the Senate shall, in the presence of the Senate and House of Representatives, open all the certificates and the votes shall then be counted;—The person having the greatest number of votes for President, shall be the President, if such number be a majority of the whole number of Electors appointed; and if no person have such majority, then from the persons having the highest numbers not exceeding three on the list of those voted for as President, the House of Representatives shall choose immediately, by ballot, the President. But in choosing the President, the votes shall be taken by states, the representation from each state having one vote; a quorum for this purpose shall consist of a member or members from two-thirds of the states, and a majority of all the states shall be necessary to a choice. And if the House of Representatives shall not choose a President whenever the right of choice shall devolve upon them, before the fourth day of March next following, then the Vice-President shall act as President, as in the case of the death or other constitutional disability of the President.14 —The person having the greatest number of votes as Vice-President, shall be the Vice-President, if such number be a majority of the whole number of Electors *appointed, and if no person have a majority, then from the two highest numbers on the list, the Senate shall choose the Vice-President; a quorum for the purpose shall consist of two-thirds of the whole number of Senators, and a majority of the whole number shall be necessary to a choice. But no person constitutionally ineligible to the office of President shall be eligible to that of Vice-President of the United States.*

Amendment 13 - Slavery and Involuntary Servitude

Neither slavery nor involuntary servitude, except as a punishment for crime whereof the party shall have been duly convicted, shall exist within the United States, or any place subject to their jurisdiction.

Congress shall have power to enforce this article by appropriate legislation.

Amendment 14 - Rights Guaranteed: Privileges and Immunities of Citizenship, Due Process, and Equal Protection

1: All persons born or naturalized in the United States, and subject to the jurisdiction thereof, are citizens of the United States and of the State wherein they reside. No State shall make or enforce any law which shall abridge the privileges or immunities of citizens of the United States; nor shall any State deprive any person of life, liberty, or property, without due process of law; nor deny to any person within its jurisdiction the equal protection of the laws.

2: Representatives shall be apportioned among the several States according to their respective numbers, counting the whole number of persons in each State, excluding Indians not taxed. But when the right to vote at any election for the choice of electors for President and Vice President of the United States, Representatives in Congress, the Executive and Judicial officers of a State, or the members of the Legislature thereof, is denied to any of the male inhabitants of such State, being twenty-one years of age,15 and citizens of the United States, or in any way abridged, except for participation in rebellion, or other crime, the basis of representation therein shall be reduced in the proportion which the number of such male citizens shall bear to the whole number of male citizens twenty-one years of age in such State.

3: No person shall be a Senator or Representative in Congress, or elector of President and Vice President, or hold any office, civil or military, under the United States, or under any State, who, having previously taken an oath, as a member of Congress, or as an officer of the United States, or as a member of any State legislature, or as an executive or judicial officer of any State, to support the Constitution of the United States, shall have engaged in insurrection or rebellion against the same, or given aid or comfort to the enemies thereof. But Congress may by a vote of two-thirds of each House, remove such disability.

4: The validity of the public debt of the United States, authorized by law, including debts incurred for payment of pensions and bounties for services in suppressing insurrection or rebellion, shall not be questioned. But neither the United States nor any State shall assume or pay any debt or obligation incurred in aid of insurrection or rebellion against the United States, or any claim for the loss or emancipation of any slave; but all such debts, obligations and claims shall be held illegal and void.

5: The Congress shall have power to enforce, by appropriate legislation, the provisions of this article.

Amendment 15 - Rights of Citizens to Vote

The right of citizens of the United States to vote shall not be denied or abridged by the United States or by any State on account of race, color, or previous condition of servitude.

The Congress shall have power to enforce this article by appropriate legislation.

Amendment 16 - Income Tax

The Congress shall have power to lay and collect taxes on incomes, from whatever source derived, without apportionment among the several States, and without regard to any census or enumeration.   ratified #16   affects 2

Amendment 17 - Popular Election of Senators

1: The Senate of the United States shall be composed of two Senators from each State, elected by the people thereof, for six years; and each Senator shall have one vote. The electors in each State shall have the qualifications requisite for electors of the most numerous branch of the State legislatures.

2: When vacancies happen in the representation of any State in the Senate, the executive authority of such State shall issue writs of election to fill such vacancies: Provided, That the legislature of any State may empower the executive thereof to make temporary appointments until the people fill the vacancies by election as the legislature may direct.

3: This amendment shall not be so construed as to affect the election or term of any Senator chosen before it becomes valid as part of the Constitution.

Amendment 18 - Prohibition of Intoxicating Liquors

1: After one year from the ratification of this article the manufacture, sale, or transportation of intoxicating liquors within, the importation thereof into, or the exportation thereof from the United States and all territory subject to the jurisdiction thereof for beverage purposes is hereby prohibited.

2: The Congress and the several States shall have concurrent power to enforce this article by appropriate legislation.

3: This article shall be inoperative unless it shall have been ratified as an amendment to the Constitution by the legislatures of the several States, as provided in the Constitution, within seven years from the date of the submission hereof to the States by the Congress.

Amendment 19 - Women's Suffrage Rights

The right of citizens of the United States to vote shall not be denied or abridged by the United States or by any State on account of sex.

Congress shall have power to enforce this article by appropriate legislation.

Amendment 20 - Terms of President, Vice President, Members of Congress: Presidential Vacancy

1: The terms of the President and Vice President shall end at noon on the 20th day of January, and the terms of Senators and Representatives at noon on the 3d day of January, of the years in which such terms would have ended if this article had not been ratified; and the terms of their successors shall then begin.

2: The Congress shall assemble at least once in every year, and such meeting shall begin at noon on the 3d day of January, unless they shall by law appoint a different day.

3: If, at the time fixed for the beginning of the term of the President, the President elect shall have died, the Vice President elect shall become President. If a President shall not have been chosen before the time fixed for the beginning of his term, or if the President elect shall have failed to qualify, then the Vice President elect shall act as President until a President shall have qualified; and the Congress may by law provide for the case wherein neither a President elect nor a Vice President elect shall have qualified, declaring who shall then act as President, or the manner in which one who is to act shall be selected, and such person shall act accordingly until a President or Vice President shall have qualified.

4: The Congress may by law provide for the case of the death of any of the persons from whom the House of Representatives may choose a President whenever the right of choice shall have devolved upon them, and for the case of the death of any of the persons from whom the Senate may choose a Vice President whenever the right of choice shall have devolved upon them.   affects 9

5: Sections 1 and 2 shall take effect on the 15th day of October following the ratification of this article.

6: This article shall be inoperative unless it shall have been ratified as an amendment to the Constitution by the legislatures of three-fourths of the several States within seven years from the date of its submission.   ratified #20

Amendment 21 - Repeal of Eighteenth Amendment

1: The eighteenth article of amendment to the Constitution of the United States is hereby repealed.

2: The transportation or importation into any State, Territory, or possession of the United States for delivery or use therein of intoxicating liquors, in violation of the laws thereof, is hereby prohibited.

3: This article shall be inoperative unless it shall have been ratified as an amendment to the Constitution by conventions in the several States, as provided in the Constitution, within seven years from the date of the submission hereof to the States by the Congress.

Amendment 22 - Presidential Tenure

1: No person shall be elected to the office of the President more than twice, and no person who has held the office of President, or acted as President, for more than two years of a term to which some other person was elected President shall be elected to the office of the President more than once. But this article shall not apply to any person holding the office of President when this article was proposed by the Congress, and shall not prevent any person who may be holding the office of President, or acting as President, during the term within which this article becomes operative from holding the office of President or acting as President during the remainder of such term.

2: This article shall be inoperative unless it shall have been ratified as an amendment to the Constitution by the legislatures of three-fourths of the several states within seven years from the date of its submission to the states by the Congress.

Amendment 23 - Presidential Electors for the District of Columbia

1: The District constituting the seat of government of the United States shall appoint in such manner as the Congress may direct: A number of electors of President and Vice President equal to the whole number of Senators and Representatives in Congress to which the District would be entitled if it were a state, but in no event more than the least populous state; they shall be in addition to those appointed by the states, but they shall be considered, for the purposes of the election of President and Vice President, to be electors appointed by a state; and they shall meet in the District and perform such duties as provided by the twelfth article of amendment.

2: The Congress shall have power to enforce this article by appropriate legislation.

Amendment 24 - Abolition of Poll Tax Qualification in Federal Elections

1. The right of citizens of the United States to vote in any primary or other election for President or Vice President, for electors for President or Vice President, or for Senator or Representative in Congress, shall not be denied or abridged by the United States or any state by reason of failure to pay any poll tax or other tax.

2. The Congress shall have power to enforce this article by appropriate legislation.

Amendment 25 - Presidential Vacancy, Disability, and Inability

1: In case of the removal of the President from office or of his death or resignation, the Vice President shall become President.

2: Whenever there is a vacancy in the office of the Vice President, the President shall nominate a Vice President who shall take office upon confirmation by a majority vote of both Houses of Congress.

3: Whenever the President transmits to the President pro tempore of the Senate and the Speaker of the House of Representatives his written declaration that he is unable to discharge the powers and duties of his office, and until he transmits to them a written declaration to the contrary, such powers and duties shall be discharged by the Vice President as Acting President.

4: Whenever the Vice President and a majority of either the principal officers of the executive departments or of such other body as Congress may by law provide, transmit to the President pro tempore of the Senate and the Speaker of the House of Representatives their written declaration that the President is unable to discharge the powers and duties of his office, the Vice President shall immediately assume the powers and duties of the office as Acting President.

Thereafter, when the President transmits to the President pro tempore of the Senate and the Speaker of the House of Representatives his written declaration that no inability exists, he shall resume the powers and duties of his office unless the Vice President and a majority of either the principal officers of the executive department or of such other body as Congress may by law provide, transmit within four days to the President pro tempore of the Senate and the Speaker of the House of Representatives their written declaration that the President is unable to discharge the powers and duties of his office. Thereupon Congress shall decide the issue, assembling within forty-eight hours for that purpose if not in session. If the Congress, within twenty-one days after receipt of the latter written declaration, or, if Congress is not in session, within twenty-one days after Congress is required to assemble, determines by two-thirds vote of both Houses that the President is unable to discharge the powers and duties of his office, the Vice President shall continue to discharge the same as Acting President; otherwise, the President shall resume the powers and duties of his office.

Amendment 26 - Reduction of Voting Age Qualification

1: The right of citizens of the United States, who are 18 years of age or older, to vote, shall not be denied or abridged by the United States or any state on account of age.

2: The Congress shall have the power to enforce this article by appropriate legislation.

Amendment 27 - Congressional Pay Limitation

No law varying the compensation for the services of the Senators and Representatives shall take effect until an election of Representatives shall have intervened.

(End of Amendments)

Appendix II – Resources

Term Years	President	Party	Senate	Dem	Rep	Other	Vacant	House	Dem	Rep	Other	Vacant
1789-1797	George Washington	None	No Data					No Data				
1797-1801	John Adams	Federalist										
1799-1801												
1801-1809	Thomas Jefferson	Dem-Rep										
1803-1805												
1805-1807												
1807-1809												
1809-1817	James Madison	Dem-Rep										
1811-1813												
1813-1815												
1815-1817												
1817-1825	James Monroe	Dem-Rep										
1919-1821												
1821-1823												
1823-1825												
1825-1829	John Q. Adams	Dem-Rep										
1827-1829												
1829-1837	Andrew Jackson	Dem										
1831-1833												
1833-1835												
1835-1837												
1837-1841	Martin Van Buren	Dem										
1839-1841												
1841	William Harrison	Whig										
1841-1845	John Tyler	Whig										
1843-1845												
1845-1849	James Knox Polk	Dem										
1847-1849												
1849-1850	Zachary Taylor	Whig										
1850-1853	Millard Fillmore	Whig										
1855-1857	Franklin Pierce	Dem	62	42	15	5	-	234	83	108	43	-
1857-1859	James Buchanan	Dem	64	39	20	5	-	237	131	92	14	-
1859-1861			66	38	26	2	-	237	101	113	23	-
1861-1863	Abraham Lincoln	Rep	50	11	31	7	1	178	42	106	28	2
1863-1865			51	12	39	-	-	183	80	103	-	-
1865-1867	Andrew Johnson	Rep	52	10	42	-	-	191	46	145	-	-
1867-1869			53	11	42	-	-	193	49	143	-	1
1869-1871	Ulysses S. Grant	Rep	74	11	61	-	2	243	73	170	-	-
1871-1873			74	17	57	-	-	243	104	139	-	-
1873-1875			74	19	54	-	1	293	88	203	-	2
1875-1877			76	29	46	-	1	293	181	107	3	2
1877-1879	Rutherford B. Hayes	Rep	76	36	39	1	-	293	156	137	-	-
1879-1881			76	43	33	-	-	293	150	128	14	1
1881-1883	James A. Garfield	Rep	76	37	37	2	-	293	130	152	11	-
1883-1885	Chester A. Arthur	Rep	76	36	40	-	-	325	200	119	6	-
1885-1887	Stephen G. Cleveland	Dem	76	34	41	-	1	325	182	140	2	1
1887-1889			76	37	39	-	-	325	170	151	4	-
1889-1891	Benjamin Harrison	Rep	84	37	47	-	-	330	156	173	1	-
1891-1893			88	39	47	2	-	333	231	88	14	-
1893-1895	Stephen G. Cleveland	Dem	88	44	38	3	3	356	220	126	10	-
1895-1897			88	39	44	5	-	357	104	246	7	-
1897-1899	William McKinley	Rep	90	34	46	10	-	357	134	206	16	1
1899-1901			90	26	53	11	-	357	163	185	9	-
1901-1903	Theodore Roosevelt	Rep	90	29	56	3	2	357	153	198	5	1
1903-1905			90	32	58	-	-	386	178	207	-	1
1905-1907			90	32	58	-	-	386	136	250	-	-
1907-1909			92	29	61	-	2	386	164	222	-	-

U.S. Presidency & Congress (By Party) 1776 - 1909

A

Term Years	President	Party	Senate	Dem	Rep	Other	Vacant	House	Dem	Rep	Other	Vacant
1909-1911	William H. Taft	Rep	92	32	59	-	1	391	172	219	-	-
1911-1913			92	42	49	-	1	391	228	162	1	-
1913-1915	Woodrow Wilson	Dem	96	51	44	1	-	435	290	127	18	-
1915-1917			96	56	39	1	-	435	231	193	8	3
1917-1919			96	53	42	1	-	435	210	216	9	-
1919-1921			96	47	48	1	-	435	191	237	7	-
1921-1923	Warren G. Harding	Rep	96	37	59	-	-	435	132	300	1	2
1923-1925	Calvin Coolidge	Rep	96	43	51	2	-	435	207	225	3	-
1925-1927			96	40	54	1	1	435	183	247	5	-
1927-1929			96	47	48	1	-	435	195	237	3	-
1929-1931	Herbert Clark Hoover	Rep	96	39	56	1	-	435	163	267	1	4
1931-1933			96	47	48	1	-	435	216	218	1	-
1933-1935	Franklin D. Roosevelt	Dem	96	59	36	1	-	435	313	117	5	-
1935-1937			96	69	25	2	-	435	322	103	10	-
1937-1939			96	75	17	4	-	435	333	89	13	-
1939-1941			96	69	23	4	-	435	262	169	4	-
1941-1943			96	66	28	2	-	435	267	162	6	-
1943-1945			96	57	38	1	-	435	222	209	4	-
1945-1947	Harry S. Truman	Dem	96	57	38	1	-	435	243	190	2	-
1947-1949			96	45	51	-	-	435	188	246	1	-
1949-1951			96	54	42	-	-	435	263	171	1	-
1951-1953			96	48	47	1	-	435	234	199	2	-
1953-1955	Dwight D. Eisenhower	Rep	96	46	48	2	-	435	213	221	1	-
1955-1957			96	48	47	1	-	435	232	203	-	-
1957-1959			96	49	47	-	-	435	234	201	-	-
1959-1961			98	64	34	-	-	4363	283	153	-	-
1961-1963	John F. Kennedy	Dem	100	64	36	-	-	4374	262	175	-	-
1963-1965	Lyndon B. Johnson	Dem	100	67	33	-	-	435	258	176	-	1
1965-1967			100	68	32	-	-	435	295	140	-	-
1967-1969			100	64	36	-	-	435	248	187	-	-
1969-1971	Richard M. Nixon	Rep	100	58	42	-	-	435	243	192	-	-
1971-1973			100	54	44	2	-	435	255	180	-	-
1973-1975	Gerald R. Ford	Rep	100	56	42	2	-	435	242	192	1	-
1975-1977			100	61	37	2	-	435	291	144	-	-
1977-1979	James Carter, Jr.	Dem	100	61	38	1	-	435	292	143	-	-
1979-1981			100	58	41	1	-	435	277	158	-	-
1981-1983	Ronald W. Reagan	Rep	100	46	53	1	-	435	242	192	1	-
1983-1985			100	46	54	-	-	435	269	166	-	-
1985-1987			100	47	53	-	-	435	253	182	-	-
1987-1989			100	55	45	-	-	435	258	177	-	-
1989-1991	George H. W. Bush	Rep	100	55	45	-	-	435	260	175	-	-
1991-1993			100	56	44	-	-	435	267	167	1	-
1993-1995	William J. Clinton	Dem	100	57	43	-	-	435	258	176	1	-
1995-1997			100	48	52	-	-	435	204	230	1	-
1997-1999			100	45	55	-	-	435	207	226	2	-
1999-2001			100	45	55	-	-	435	211	223	1	-
2001-2003	George W. Bush	Rep	100	50	50	-	-	435	212	221	2	-
2003-2005			100	48	51	1	-	435	205	229	1	-
2005-2007			100	44	55	1	-	435	202	231	1	1
2007-2009			100	49	49	2	-	435	233	198	-	4
2009-2011	Barack Obama	Dem	100	57	41	2	2	435	256	178	-	1
2011-2013			100	51	47	2	—	435	193	242	-	-
2013-2015			100	54	45	1	—	435	201	234	—	-
2015-2017			100	44	54	2	—	435	188	246	—	1
2017-2019	Donald Trump	Rep	100	45	52	2	—	435	235	198	—	2
2019-2021			100	45	52	2	—	435	234	199	1	1

U.S. Presidency & Congress (By Party) 1909 - Present

State	Democrat Senator	Age	Years in off	Term Exp	Previous Office & Occupation
Alabama	Doug Jones	65	2.0	2020 (Spec)	U.S. Attorney for the Northern District of AL, Lawyer
Arizona	Kyrsten Sinema	43	1.0	2024	U.S. House, AR Senate, AR House, Social worker, Political Activist
California	Kamala Harris	54	3.0	2022	A.G. of CA, San Francisco District Attorney, Lawyer
California	Dianne Feinstein	86	27.2	2024	Mayor of San Fran, San Fran Board, CA Women's Parole Board, Non-profit Org. fellow
Colorado	Michael Bennet	54	10.9	2022	Denver Schools Super., CoS Denver Mayor, Lawyer, Inv. Comp. Exec., School Administrator
Connecticut	Chris Murphy	46	7.0	2024	U.S. House, CT Senate, Connecticut House, Lawyer, Political campaign manager
Connecticut	Richard Blumenthal	73	9.0	2022	CT A.G., CT Senate, CT House, US Attorney, USMC Reserve, Senate Staff, Lawyer
Delaware	Chris Coons	56	9.1	2020	New Castle County Exec, Member, New Castle Cnty Council, Nonprofit Org. Exec, Lawyer
Delaware	Tom Carper	72	19.0	2024	Govr. of DE, U.S House, DE Treasurer, U.S. Navy officer, DE Office of Economic Dev.
Hawaii	Mazie Hirono	71	7.0	2024	U.S. House, HA House, Lieutenant Govr. of HA, Lawyer
Hawaii	Brian Schatz	46	7.0	2022	Lieutenant Govr of HA, HA House, Nonprofit Exec
Illinois	Tammy Duckworth	51	3.0	2022	U.S. House, U.S. Assist. Sec. of VA, IL Dir. of VA, ANG Officer, Staff Supervisor, Rotary Int
Illinois	Dick Durbin	74	23.0	2020	U.S. House, Lawyer, Prof.
Maryland	Chris Van Hollen	60	3.0	2022	U.S. House, MD General Assembly, U.S. Senate staff member, Govr.'s Advisor, Lawyer
Maryland	Ben Cardin	75	13.0	2024	U.S. House, Speaker of the MD House of Delegates, Lawyer
Massachusetts	Ed Markey	73	6.5	2024	U.S. House, Massachusetts House, United States Army Reserve, Lawyer
Massachusetts	Elizabeth Warren	70	7.0	2024	Congress Oversight Panel Chair, Spec. Advisor, Lawyer, Prof., Research Assoc., Nonprof. Exec
Michigan	Gary Peters	60	5.0	2020	U.S. House, MI Senate, U.S. Navy Reserve officer, Fin. Advisor, Lawyer, College Prof.
Michigan	Debbie Stabenow	69	19.0	2024	U.S. House, MI House, MI Senate, Social worker, Leadership training consultant
Minnesota	Tina Smith	61	2.0	2020	Lieutenant Govr. of MN, Public relations consultant, Nonprofit Exec, Govr.'s CoS
Minnesota	Amy Klobuchar	59	13.0	2024	Hennepin County, MN Attorney, Lawyer
Montana	Jon Tester	63	13.0	2024	MN Senate Pres., Big Sandy, MN School Board, Music teacher, Farmer
Nevada	Jacky Rosen	62	1.0	2024	U.S. House, Computer programmer, Software Developer, Designer, Consultant
Nevada	Catherine Cortez Masto	55	3.0	2022	NA A.G., Lawyer
New Hampshire	Maggie Hassan	61	3.0	2022	Govr. of NH, NH Senate, Lawyer
New Hampshire	Jeanne Shaheen	72	11.0	2020	Govr. of NH, NH Senate, Teacher, Entrepreneur
New Jersey	Cory Booker	50	6.2	2020	Mayor of Newark, NJ, Newark Municipal Council, Lawyer
New Jersey	Bob Menendez	65	14.0	2024	U.S. House, NJ General Assembly, NJ Senate, Lawyer
New Mexico	Martin Heinrich	47	7.0	2024	U.S. House, Albuquerque City Council, Nonprofit Exec, Conultant
New Mexico	Tom Udall	71	11.0	2020	U.S. House, A.G. of NM, Assist. U.S. Attorney, Lawyer
New York	Kirsten Gillibrand	52	10.9	2024	U.S. House, U.S. HUD special counsel, Lawyer
New York	Chuck Schumer	68	21.0	2022	U.S. House, NY State Assembly, Lawyer
Ohio	Sherrod Brown	66	13.0	2024	U.S. House, OH Sec. of State, OH House, Teacher
Oregon	Jeff Merkley	62	11.0	2020	OR House Speaker, Nonprofit Exec, CBO analyst, Defense Department
Oregon	Ron Wyden	70	23.9	2022	U.S. House, Teacher, Nonprofit Org. Exec
Pennsylvania	Bob Casey Jr.	59	13.0	2024	PA Treasurer, PA Auditor, Teacher, lawyer
Rhode Island	Sheldon Whitehouse	63	13.0	2024	A.G. of RI, United States Attorney, Lawyer
Rhode Island	Jack Reed	69	23.0	2020	U.S. House, RI Senate, Lawyer, Army Reserve officer, Army officer
Vermont	Patrick Leahy	79	45.0	2022	Chittenden County, VT State's Attorney, Lawyer, Farmer, College Prof.
Virginia	Tim Kaine	61	7.0	2024	Govr. of VA, Lt. Govr. of VA, DNC Chair, Mayor of Richmond, Missionary, Lawyer, Teacher
Virginia	Mark Warner	64	11.0	2020	Govr. of VA, VA Democratic Party Chair, Businessman, Venture capitalist
Washington	Maria Cantwell	60	19.0	2024	U.S. House, WA House, Marketing V.P.
Washington	Patty Murray	68	27.0	2022	WA Senate, School Board, Teacher
West Virginia	Joe Manchin	72	9.1	2024	Govr. of WV, Sec. of State of WV, WV House, WV Senate, Corp. Exec
Wisconsin	Tammy Baldwin	57	7.0	2024	U.S. House, WI Assembly, Lawyer
Maine	Angus King	75	7.0	2024	Govr. of ME, Lawyer, Senate Staff, Business Founder, Corp. Exec, Public TV Host
Vermont	Bernie Sanders	78	13.0	2024	U.S. House, Mayor of Burlington, VT, Filmmaker, Carpenter, Writer, Researcher
Average Years in Office			11.5		

U.S. Senators as of 2019 (Democrat)

State	Democrat Senator	Age	Years in off	Term Exp	Previous Office & Occupation
Alabama	Richard Shelby	85	33.0	2022	U.S. House, AL Senate, Lawyer
Alaska	Dan Sullivan	54	5.0	2020	AK A.G., Assist. Sec. of State for Economic/Business Affairs, U.S. Marine officer, Lawyer
Alaska	Lisa Murkowski	62	17.0	2022	AK House, Lawyer
Arizona	Martha McSally	53	1.0 2020 (Spec		U.S. House, U.S. Air Force officer
Arkansas	Tom Cotton	42	5.0	2020	U.S. House, Lawyer, US Army Officer
Arkansas	John Boozman	68	9.0	2022	U.S. House, Rogers Public Schools Board, Optometrist
Colorado	Cory Gardner	45	5.0	2020	U.S. House, CO House of, Lawyer, Businessman
Florida	Rick Scott	66	1.0	2024	Govr. of FL, Lawyer, Columbia/HCA CEO, Venture Capitalist
Florida	Marco Rubio	48	9.0	2022	FL House Speaker, West Miami, FL City Commission, Lawyer
Georgia	David Perdue	69	5.0	2020	None, Corp. Exec
Georgia	Johnny Isakson	74	15.0	2022	U.S. House, GA House, GA State Senate, Real estate broker
Idaho	Jim Risch	76	11.0	2020	Govr. of ID, Lieutenant Govr. of ID, ID Pres. Pro Temp, Prof., Rancher, Nonprofit Exec
Idaho	Mike Crapo	68	21.0	2022	U.S. House, ID Senate, Lawyer
Indiana	Mike Braun	65	1.0	2024	IN House, Businessman
Indiana	Todd Young	47	3.0	2022	U.S. House, Marine Corps officer, Professor, Consultant
Iowa	Joni Ernst	49	5.0	2020	IA Senate, Farmer, Army N.G. Officer
Iowa	Chuck Grassley	86	39.0	2022	U.S. House, IA House
Kansas	Jerry Moran	65	9.0	2022	U.S. House, KS Senate, Banker, Lawyer
Kansas	Pat Roberts	83	23.0	2020	U.S. House, USMC Officer, Journalist, U.S. Senate staff member, U.S. House staff member
Kentucky	Rand Paul	56	9.0	2022	None, Ophthalmologist
Kentucky	Mitch McConnell	77	35.0	2020	U.S. DoJ Legislative Affairs, County Judge/ Exec, Lawyer, US Senate Staff, U.S. Senate staff
Louisiana	John Kennedy	67	3.0	2022	LA Treasurer, Sec., LA Department of Revenue, Magazine editor, Lawyer, Prof., Govr Staff
Louisiana	Bill Cassidy	62	5.0	2020	U.S. House, LA Senate, Physician
Maine	Susan Collins	66	23.0	2020	MA Dep Treas, ME Fin. Reg Commiss, House Staff, Senate Staff, SBA Reg Dir., Nonprofit Exec
Mississippi	Cindy Hyde-Smith	60	1.7	2020	MS Commissioner of Agriculture and Commerce, MS Senate, Farmer
Mississippi	Roger Wicker	68	12.0	2024	U.S. House, MS Senate, U.S. Air Force officer/Judge Advocate, U.S. House Staff, Lawyer
Missouri	Josh Hawley	39	1.0	2024	A.G of MO, Lawyer
Missouri	Roy Blunt	69	9.0	2022	U.S. House, MO Sec. of State, Green County Clerk, University Pres.
Montana	Steve Daines	57	5.0	2020	U.S. House, Businessman
Nebraska	Ben Sasse	47	5.0	2020	Assist. Sec. for Planning/Evaluation (HHS), Mgmt. consultant, Nonprofit Exec, Prof., Univ. Pres.
Nebraska	Deb Fischer	68	7.0	2024	NE Legislature, Rancher
North Carolin	Thom Tillis	59	5.0	2020	Speaker of the NC House, Business consultant
North Carolin	Richard Burr	63	15.0	2022	U.S. House, Sales manager, Nonprofit Org. Exec
North Dakota	Kevin Cramer	58	1.0	2024	U.S. House, ND Public Svcs Commiss, State Tourism Dir., State Econ Dir., State Party Chair
North Dakota	John Hoeven	62	9.0	2022	Govr. of ND, Banker
Ohio	Rob Portman	63	9.0	2022	U.S. House, U.S. Trade Representative, Dir. of OMB, Lawyer
Oklahoma	James Lankford	51	5.0	2022	U.S. House, Nonprofit program Dir.
Oklahoma	Jim Inhofe	84	25.1	2020	U.S. House, Mayor of Tulsa OK, OK Senate, OK House, Businessman, Real Estate Dev. Exec
Pennsylvania	Pat Toomey	57	9.0	2022	U.S. House, Currency trader, Restaurant owner
South Carolir	Tim Scott	54	7.0	2022	U.S. House, SC House, Charleston County Council, Insurance agent, Fin. adviser
South Carolir	Lindsey Graham	64	17.0	2020	U.S. House, SC House, Lawyer, Air Force Reserve officer
South Dakota	Mike Rounds	64	5.0	2020	Govr. of SD, SD Senate, Businessman
South Dakota	John Thune	58	15.0	2022	U.S. House, SD Republican Party Exec Dir., Nonprofit Exec, State Railroad Dir.
Tennessee	Marsha Blackburn	67	1.0	2024	U.S. House, TN Senate, Consultant, State Media Exec Dir., County Party Chair
Tennessee	Lamar Alexander	79	17.0	2020	Govr. of TN, U.S. Sec. of Education, Senate Staff, lawyer, Businessman
Texas	Ted Cruz	48	7.0	2024	U.S. Assoc. Deputy AG, TX Solicitor General, Lawyer
Texas	John Cornyn	67	17.1	2020	San Antonio District Judge, TX Attorney General, TX Supreme Court, Lawyer
Utah	Mitt Romney	72	1.0	2024	Govr. of Massachusetts, Businessman
Utah	Mike Lee	48	9.0	2022	Assist. United States Attorney, Lawyer, Govr's general counsel
West Virginia	Shelley Moore Capit	65	5.0	2020	U.S. House, WV House of Delegates, College career counselor, Dir. for Board of Regents
Wisconsin	Ron Johnson	64	9.0	2022	None, Accountant, Corp. Exec
Wyoming	John Barrasso	67	12.5	2024	WY Senate, Orthopedic surgeon, Med CoS, Nonprofit Exec
Wyoming	Mike Enzi	75	23.0	2020	WY House, WY Senate, Nonprofit Org. Exec, Accountant, CEO, Member, Air N.G.
Average Years in Office			10.5		

U.S. Senators as of 2019 (Republican)

State	Total	# Dem	% Dem	# Rep	% Rep	# Ind/Open
Alabama	7	1	14%	6	86%	
Alaska	1	0	0%	1	100%	
Arizona	9	5	56%	4	44%	
Arkansas	4	0	0%	4	100%	
California	53	46	87%	7	13%	
Colorado	7	4	57%	3	43%	
Connecticut	5	5	100%	0	0%	
Delaware	1	1	100%	0	0%	
Florida	27	13	48%	14	52%	
Georgia	14	5	36%	9	64%	
Hawaii	2	2	100%	0	0%	
Idaho	2	0	0%	2	100%	
Illinois	18	13	72%	5	28%	
Indiana	9	2	22%	7	78%	
Iowa	4	3	75%	1	25%	
Kansas	4	1	25%	3	75%	
Kentucky	6	1	17%	5	83%	
Louisiana	6	1	17%	5	83%	
Maine	2	2	100%	0	0%	
Maryland	8	7	88%	1	13%	
Massachusetts	9	9	100%	0	0%	
Michigan	14	7	50%	6	43%	1
Minnesota	8	5	63%	3	38%	
Mississippi	4	1	25%	3	75%	
Missouri	8	2	25%	6	75%	
Montana	1	0	0%	1	100%	
Nebraska	3	0	0%	3	100%	
Nevada	4	3	75%	1	25%	
New Hampshire	2	2	100%	0	0%	
New Jersey	12	11	92%	1	8%	
New Mexico	3	3	100%	0	0%	
New York	27	22	81%	4	15%	1
North Carolina	13	3	23%	10	77%	
North Dakota	1	0	0%	1	100%	
Ohio	16	4	25%	12	75%	
Oklahoma	5	1	20%	4	80%	
Oregon	5	4	80%	1	20%	
Pennsylvania	18	9	50%	9	50%	
Rhode Island	2	2	100%	0	0%	
South Carolina	7	2	29%	5	71%	
South Dakota	1	0	0%	1	100%	
Tennessee	9	2	22%	7	78%	
Texas	36	13	36%	23	64%	
Utah	4	1	25%	3	75%	
Vermont	1	1	100%	0	0%	
Virginia	11	8	73%	3	27%	
Washington	10	7	70%	3	30%	
West Virginia	3	0	0%	3	100%	
Wisconsin	8	3	38%	4	50%	1
Wyoming	1	0	0%	1	100%	
Totals	435	237	48%	195	51%	3
	Total	# Dem	% Dem	# Rep	% Rep	# Ind/Open

U.S. House of Representatives by State

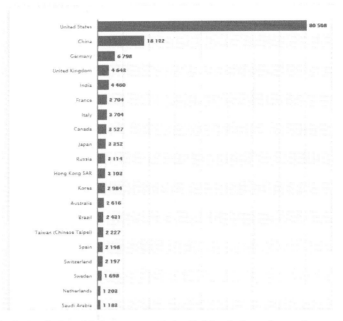

United States			80 508
China		18 132	
Germany	6 798		
United Kingdom	4 642		
India	4 460		
France	2 704		
Italy	2 704		
Canada	2 527		
Japan	2 352		
Russia	2 114		
Hong Kong SAR	2 102		
Korea	2 984		
Australia	2 616		
Brazil	2 431		
Taiwan (Chinese Taipei)	2 227		
Spain	2 198		
Switzerland	2 197		
Sweden	1 698		
Netherlands	1 203		
Saudi Arabia	1 183		

Number of ultra high net worth individuals in selected countries in 2019
Statist 2019 Data

2016 Super PAC Mega Donors
Washington Post - Nov 2016

NAME	ABOUT	PARTY LEANING	DONATION
Tom Steyer	Hedge fund founder	Democratic	$66.3 million
Miriam & Sheldon Adelson	Medical professional; Casino magnate	Republican	$52.7 million
S. Donald Sussman	Hedge fund manager	Democratic	$36.8 million
Fred Eychaner	Media company owner	Democratic	$33.1 million
Robert Mercer	Technologist and hedge fund manager	Republican	$21.2 million
Michael Bloomberg	Former New York City mayor	Independent	$20.1 million
Paul Singer	Hedge fund executive	Republican	$19.8 million
Marilyn & James Simons	Hedge fund manager	Democratic	$18.5 million
George Soros	Hedge fund founder	Democratic	$17.5 million
Dustin Moskovitz & Cari Tuna	Philanthropist; Facebook co-founder	Democratic	$17.3 million
M.K. & J.B. Pritzker	Investor; philanthropist	Democratic	$16.4 million
Maurice "Hank" Greenberg	Former chairman of AIG	Republican	$15.3 million
Elizabeth & Richard Uihlein	Founders of Wisconsin-based packaging company	Republican	$14.9 million
Marlene & Joe Ricketts	Philanthropist; TD Ameritrade founder	Republican	$14.4 million
Ronald Cameron	Arkansas-based poultry company owner	Republican	$13.9 million
Kenneth C. Griffin	Hedge fund manager	Republican	$11.6 million
Warren Stephens	Arkansas-based investment banker	Republican	$11.2 million
Cheryl & Haim Saban	Women's advocate/author; Univision chairman	Democratic	$11.1 million
Daniel Abraham	Slim-Fast founder	Democratic	$10 million

2016 Super PAC Mega Donors

No.	Name	Net worth (USD)	Age	Nationality	Source(s) of wealth
1 —	Jeff Bezos	$131 billion ▲	55	United States	Amazon
2 —	Bill Gates	$96.5 billion ▲	63	United States	Microsoft
3 —	Warren Buffett	$82.5 billion ▼	88	United States	Berkshire Hathaway
4 —	Bernard Arnault	$76 billion ▲	70	France	LVMH
5 ▲	Carlos Slim	$64 billion ▼	79	Mexico	América Móvil, Grupo Carso
6 —	Amancio Ortega	$62.7 billion ▼	82	Spain	Inditex, Zara
7 ▲	Larry Ellison	$62.5 billion ▲	74	United States	Oracle Corporation
8 ▼	Mark Zuckerberg	$62.3 billion ▼	34	United States	Facebook
9 ▲	Michael Bloomberg	$55.5 billion ▲	77	United States	Bloomberg L.P.
10 ▲	Larry Page	$50.8 billion ▲	45	United States	Alphabet Inc.

Forbes 2019 List of the World's Wealthiest

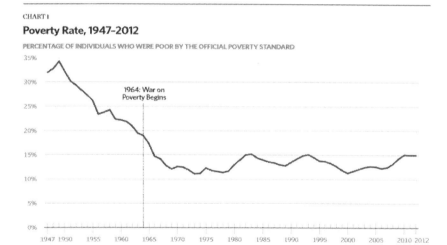

BACKGROUNDER | NO. 2955
SEPTEMBER 15, 2014

CHART 1

Poverty Rate, 1947–2012

PERCENTAGE OF INDIVIDUALS WHO WERE POOR BY THE OFFICIAL POVERTY STANDARD

1964: War on Poverty Begins

Sources: Figures for 1947–1958: Gordon Fisher, "Estimates of the Poverty Population Under the Current Official Definition for Years Before 1959," U.S. Department of Health and Human Services, Office of the Assistant Secretary for Planning and Evaluation, 1986. Figures for 1959–2012: U.S. Census Bureau, Current Population Survey, Annual Social and Economic Supplements, "Historical Poverty Tables—People," Table 2, https://www.census.gov/hhes/www/poverty/data/historical/people.html (accessed September 10, 2014).

BG 2955 ☎ heritage.org

Poverty Rate, 1947-2012 (Various Sources)

Rank ◆	Race ◆	Median household income (2016 US$) ◆
1	Indian	128,000[1]
2	East Asian	85,349[1]
3	White	67,865[1]
4	Native Hawaiian and Other Pacific Islander	50,987[1]
5	Hispanic or Latino (of any race)	46,882[1]
6	American Indian and Alaska Native	39,719[1]
7	Black or African American	30,555[1]

Wikipedia – 2016 Median Household Income

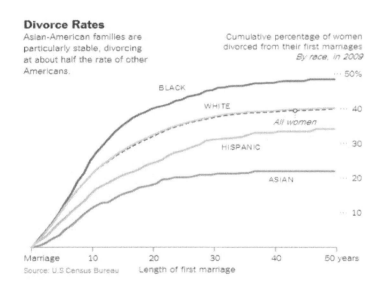

Divorce Rates

Asian-American families are particularly stable, divorcing at about half the rate of other Americans.

Cumulative percentage of women divorced from their first marriages
By race, in 2009

BLACK
WHITE
All women
HISPANIC
ASIAN

Marriage — 10 — 20 — 30 — 40 — 50 years

Source: U.S Census Bureau   Length of first marriage

Divorce is a wealth destroyer

United States Divorce Rate by Nationality

TABLE 10
Nonfatal violent incidents, by total population, victim, and offender demographic characteristics, 2017

Demographic characteristic	Population[a] Number of persons	Population[a] Percent of persons	Victim Number of incidents	Victim Percent	Offender[b] Number of incidents	Offender[b] Percent
Total	272,468,480	100%	5,179,800	100%	5,179,800	100%
Sex						
Male*	132,432,710	48.6%	2,534,130	48.9%	3,602,740	75.8%
Female	140,035,770	51.4	2,645,670	51.1	959,200 †	20.2 †
Both male and female offenders	~	~	~	~	188,770 †	4.0 †
Race/Hispanic origin[c]						
White*	171,454,370	62.9%	3,247,940	62.7%	2,230,910	49.2%
Black	32,699,520	12.0	697,590 †	13.5 †	1,112,610 †	24.5 †
Hispanic	45,481,910	16.7	853,730 †	16.5 †	647,970 †	14.3 †
Asian	16,582,080	6.1	113,850 †	2.2 †	44,090 †	1.0 †
Other[d]	6,250,600	2.3	266,690 †	5.1 †	425,050 †	9.4 †
Multiple offenders of various races[e]	~	~	~	~	74,450 †	1.6 †
Age						
12 or younger	~	~	~	~	109,280 †	2.5% †
12–17	24,911,170	9.1%	785,080 †	15.2% †	667,620 †	15.3 †
18–20*	12,599,000	4.6	443,910	8.6	327,490	7.5
21–29	40,111,370	14.7	1,064,630 †	20.6 †	900,360 †	20.6 †
30 or older	194,846,940	71.5	2,886,190 †	55.7 †	2,170,420 †	49.6 †
Multiple offenders of various ages	~	~	~	~	200,270 †	4.6 †

Note: Based on persons age 12 or older. Details may not sum to totals due to rounding and missing data for offender characteristics. An incident is a specific criminal act involving one or more victims or victimizations. Offender characteristics are based on the victims' perceptions of the offenders. See appendix table 12 for standard errors.
*Comparison group.
†Significant difference from comparison group at the 95% confidence level.
~Not applicable.
[a]NCVS population includes persons age 12 or older living in non-institutionalized residential settings in the United States.
[b]Includes incidents in which the perceived offender characteristics were reported. The sex of the offender was unknown in 8% of incidents, the race/Hispanic origin of offender was unknown in 12% of incidents, and the age of offender was unknown in 16% of incidents.
[c]Excludes persons of Hispanic/Latino origin, unless specified.
[d]Includes American Indians and Alaska Natives; Native Hawaiians and Other Pacific Islanders; and persons of two or more races.
[e]Victims perceived multiple offenders of various races or Hispanic origin.
Source: Bureau of Justice Statistics, National Crime Victimization Survey, 2017 Public-Use File.

2017 Violent Incidents (Bureau of Justice Statistics)

	BCA Caps LT effects ("Sequestration")	Obama FY 2017 FYDP Goal	Trump Campaign (9/2016)	FY 2020 Budget	FY 2024 FYDP Plan[s]
Army manpower (regular/reserve)	421,000/498,000	450,000/ 530,000	540,000/ [563,000]*	480,000/ 525,500	488,000/ 528,500
Army brigade combat teams (AC/RC)	53 (27/26)	58 (30/28)	68 (40/28)	58 (31/27)	58 (31/27)
Navy carriers	10	11	12	11	11
Navy ships	274	295	350	301	314 (355 by FY2034)
Air Force TacAir A/C (4th/5th generation)	1,015 (668/347)	1,101 (699/402)	1,310 (837/473)	1,194 (939/255)	~1,200*** (833/367)
USMC manpower	175,000	180,000	242,000 (!)**	186,200	186,400

DoD Force Structure Targets by Administration

l

CAUSE OF DEATH RANKING	All Ages		0 - 14		15 - 24		25 - 34		35 - 44		45 - 54		55 - 64		65 - 74		75 +	
	Rank	Deaths	Rank	Deaths	Rank	Deaths	Rank	Deaths	Rank	Deaths	Rank	Deaths	Rank	Deaths	Rank	Deaths	Rank	Deaths
CORONARY HEART DISEASE	1	365,699	23	41	19	109	7	939	4	4,611	1	18,697	1	49,967	1	73,182	1	218,344
LUNG DISEASE	2	155,013	28	22	38	13	36	59	29	382	13	3,509	3	17,953	3	39,023	4	94,652
STROKE	3	146,381	12	263	17	155	13	593	11	1,811	9	5,198	6	12,708	4	22,600	3	102,963
LUNG CANCERS	4	145,932	30	12	32	17	33	112	16	843	5	6,989	2	29,505	2	47,654	5	60,800
ALZHEIMERS	5	121,402	52	0	64	0	66	0	57	11	51	95	38	1,189	16	7,281	2	112,826
HYPERTENSION	6	90,075	42	3	21	89	11	682	7	2,237	7	6,183	7	12,690	6	14,793	6	53,398
DIABETES MELLITUS	7	83,563	24	41	11	248	9	823	8	2,118	6	6,409	4	14,904	5	21,344	8	37,676
POISONINGS	8	84,782	21	83	3	5,030	1	16,478	1	15,032	2	14,707	8	10,581	33	2,241	46	630
INFLUENZA & PNEUMONIA	9	55,954	10	442	14	190	18	410	18	787	20	2,023	17	5,062	14	8,799	7	38,241
COLON-RECTUM CANCERS	10	53,447	47	1	26	40	23	342	13	1,453	11	4,976	9	10,398	8	13,011	12	23,226
KIDNEY DISEASE	11	52,001	19	102	25	59	25	271	19	714	19	2,258	16	5,833	9	10,540	9	32,224
SUICIDE	12	47,168	9	522	2	6,252	2	7,948	2	7,335	3	8,561	12	7,982	23	4,620	32	3,948
ENDOCRINE DISORDERS	13	44,414	8	689	7	460	6	1,095	10	1,813	12	3,624	14	7,055	13	8,940	13	20,738
PANCREAS CANCER	14	44,011	48	1	51	3	38	56	25	470	15	2,556	11	8,633	7	13,692	15	18,600
BREAST CANCER	15	42,510	53	0	40	13	20	385	9	1,873	10	4,978	10	9,024	10	10,272	17	15,965
LIVER DISEASE	16	41,695	34	5	28	23	8	918	6	2,998	4	8,309	5	13,724	11	9,303	24	6,335
ROAD TRAFFIC ACCIDENTS	17	39,992	5	1,231	1	6,789	3	7,013	3	5,337	8	5,720	15	5,899	26	3,833	31	4,170
FALLS	18	36,338	22	55	12	212	22	351	23	522	24	1,248	25	2,760	21	4,752	11	26,438
LYMPHOMAS	19	34,377	25	35	20	99	27	230	24	477	23	1,592	18	4,714	12	8,959	16	18,271
PARKINSON'S DISEASE	20	31,963	54	0	56	1	56	4	59	7	54	60	42	714	22	4,661	10	26,516
PROSTATE CANCER	21	30,486	49	1	55	1	61	1	58	8	41	399	26	2,743	17	7,280	14	20,053
INFLAMMATORY/HEART	22	29,062	15	190	10	264	10	603	14	1,265	17	2,453	19	4,329	19	5,440	18	14,318
OTHER INJURIES	23	27,610	3	1,908	5	942	5	1,385	12	1,652	14	2,566	20	4,073	24	4,560	21	10,524
LIVER CANCER	24	27,104	26	35	29	21	34	110	31	338	21	1,847	13	7,754	15	8,580	23	8,419
LEUKEMIA	25	23,359	11	315	9	310	21	367	22	541	27	1,115	24	2,839	18	5,481	19	12,391

https://www.worldlifeexpectancy.com/usa-cause-of-death-by-age-and-gender

About the Author

 LT Daniel Wilson dedicated 22 years of service to our nation as a Naval Corpsman aboard ship, with the U.S. Marines and as a Navy UDT/SEAL with UDT-12 and SEAL Team 5. With 12 years enlisted service, Dan was promoted to the Navy's Officer ranks in Hospital Administration where he served as a Facilities Manager and Health Facilities Planner at Guantanamo Bay, Cuba, NDC Norfolk, VA, NHSO Jacksonville, FL, and eventually serving the Navy's Surgeon General in Washington D.C. as Head of Planning & Programming for Healthcare Construction initiatives.

Upon retiring from Naval service, Dan was again called on by the Navy to lead a critical initiative to design, development and implementation a standardized DoD wide Health Facilities Management Program. As the Navy's Program Manager, and eventual contract representative for Army Medical Command, Dan was critical to establishing global management throughout the DoD, working with the Veterans Administration (VA) and Civilian Health Programs. His 19 added years of service to our nation continue today.

Having a passion to encourage others to pursue a life of purpose, Dan has served his fellow man through various community, business, political and leadership initiatives. These passions eventually lead Dan into the world of authorship and internet radio (America's Champions), where he interviewed American leaders such as Dr. Ben Carson, Agent Dan Bongino, Astronaut CAPT Chris Cassidy (SEAL), Colonel/Dr. David Balt, Entrepreneur Anne Beiler (Auntie Anne's Pretzels) and many others.

Dan and his beautiful bride Robin share their time between Gettysburg, PA and the Cocoa Beach, FL areas. Current business ventures include Azure Sol, LLC and Azure Sol Publishing. Dan and Robin also make sure to take time with their grown children and two beautiful granddaughters, promoting personal and national freedom at every opportunity.

Follow LT Dan on Facebook, Twitter and at **www.ASK-Force.com**

Other Books by LT Dan Wilson

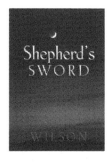   

Shepherd's Sword - 2012

The A.S.K. Force - 2014

A.S.K. America – 2016

A.S.K. for Purpose – 2018

Made in the USA
Columbia, SC
06 September 2022

66109530R00098